The *Magic* of God Bless You

Also by Sirshree

Spiritual Masterpieces - Self Realisation books for serious seekers
The Secret of Awakening
The Source of Silence : Journey Inward to the True Self
100% Karma: Learn the Art of Conscious Karma that Liberates
100% Meditation: Dip into the Stillness of Pure Awareness
You are Meditation: Discover Peace and Bliss Within
Essence of Devotion: From Devotee to Divinity
The Supreme Quest: Your search for the Truth ends there where you are
Secret of The Third Side of The Coin
Seek Forgiveness & be Free: Liberation from Karmic Bondage
Passwords to a Happy Life: The Art of Being Happy in all Situations

Self Help Treasures - Self Development books for success seekers
The Source of Health: The Key to Perfect Health Discovery
Inner Ninety Hidden Infinity: How to build your book of values
Inner 90 for Youth: The secret of reaching and staying at the peak of success
The Source for Youth: You have the power to change your life
Inner Magic: The Power of self-talk
The Power of Present: Experience the Joy of the Now
You are Not Lazy: A story of shifting from Laziness to Success
Freedom From Fear, Worry, Anger: How to be cool, calm and courageous
The Little Gita of Problem Solving: Gift of 18 Solutions to Any Problem

New Age Nuggets - Practical books on applied spirituality and self help
The Source: Power of Happy Thoughts
Secret of Happiness: Instant Happiness - Here and Now!
Help God to Help You: Whatever you do, do it with a smile
Ultimate Purpose of Success: Achieving Success in all five aspects of life
Celebrating Relationships: Bringing Love, Life, Laughter in Your Relations
Everything is a Game of Beliefs: Understanding is the Whole Thing
Detachment From Attachment: Gift of Freedom From Suffering
Emotional Freedom Through Spiritual Wisdom

Profound Parables - Fiction books containing profound truths
Beyond Life: Conversations on Life After Death
The One Above: What if God was your neighbour?
The Warrior's Mirror: The Path To Peace
Master of Siddhartha: Revealing the Truth of Life and After-life
Put Stress to Rest: Utilizing Stress to Make Progress
The Source @ Work: A Story of Inspiration from Jeeodee

SIRSHREE
Author of the
bestseller *The Source*

The
Magic
of God Bless You

Bring Health, Harmony and Happiness in Your Life
through Prayer of Wellbeing for Everyone

THE MAGIC OF GOD BLESS YOU
By **Sirshree** Tejparkhi

Copyright © Tejgyan Global Foundation
All Rights Reserved 2021

Tejgyan Global Foundation is a charitable organization
with its headquarters in Pune, India.

ISBN : 978-93-90607-39-6

Published by WOW Publishings Pvt. Ltd., India

First edition published in October 2021

Printed and bound by Trinity Academy, Pune, INDIA

This book is the translation of the Hindi book titled
"Magic of God Bless You" by Sirshree Tejparkhi.

Copyrights are reserved with Tejgyan Global Foundation and publishing rights are vested exclusively with WOW Publishings Pvt. Ltd. This book is sold subject to the condition that it shall not by way of trade or otherwise, be lent, resold, hired out, or otherwise circulated without the publisher's prior written consent in any form of binding or cover other than that in which it is published and without a similar condition including this condition being imposed on the subsequent purchaser and without limiting the rights under copyright reserved above, no part of this publication may be reproduced, stored in or introduced into a retrieval system, or transmitted, in any form, or by any means, electronic, mechanical, photocopying, recording or otherwise, without the prior written permission of both the copyright owner and the above-mentioned publisher of this book. Any person who does any unauthorized act in relation to this publication may be liable to criminal prosecution and civil claims for damages.

Although the author and publisher have made every effort to ensure accuracy of content in this book, they hereby disclaim any liability to any party for any loss, damage, or disruption caused by errors or omissions, resulting from negligence, accident, or any other cause. Readers are advised to take full responsibility to exercise discretion in understanding and applying the content of this book.

To

*the Anupam Prayer fraternity
who selflessly radiate divine healing rays
on all beings every day.*

Contents

	Preface	9
1.	The Extraordinary Tree	13
2.	The Onset of Karmic Disease	17
3.	Annihilation of Karmic Disease	21
4.	Understanding Karmic Disease	24
5.	Causes of Karmic Disease	27
6.	The Effects of Karmic Disease	32
7.	The Meaning of Healing Rays	35
8.	The Science of Healing Rays	40
9.	The Effect of Positive Words	43
10.	Whom Should We Send Healing Rays?	47
11.	Who Needs Healing Rays the Most?	51
12.	Nature – the Greatest Healer	55
13.	Qualities Required to Send Healing Rays	58
14.	The Three P's – Prescribe, Pray, and Proclaim	62
15.	Shoot the Arrows of Healing Rays	66
16.	Benefits of Healing Rays	72
17.	Improving Relationships with Healing Rays	75

18.	Changing Behavior with Healing Rays	79
19.	Sympathy and Compassion	83
20.	Contributing to the World	87
21.	Self-healing Rays and Bright-healing Rays	90
22.	Meditation to Transmit Healing Rays	94
	APPENDIX	**97**
	Opening Your Mind with Healing Rays	99
Incident 1	What to Do When You Are Anxious and Worried	102
Incident 2	What to Do When You Are Gripped by Fear	104
Incident 3	Healing Rays for Decision Making	107
Incident 4	Healing Rays for Health	110
Incident 5	Healing Rays for Food	113
Incident 6	Healing Rays for Anger	115
Incident 7	Healing Rays for Problems	118
Incident 8	Healing Rays for Inanimate Objects	120
Incident 9	Send Healing Rays Instead of Blaming	123
Incident 10	Send Healing Rays to Yourself for Your Bad Habits	125
Incident 11	Healing Rays for the World	128
Prayer 1	Compassionate Wishes for Awakening	133
Prayer 2	Compassionate Wishes for Wellbeing	135

Preface
The Profound Effect of an Exceptional Power

There is a famous story of the natives of the Solomon Islands, located in the South Pacific Ocean. Usually, cutting down large trees is an arduous task, but the native tribes of these islands would use a peculiar technique. They would gather around the tree in large numbers and loudly abuse it, scream curses at it. They would repeat this for about thirty days. After that, the tree would gradually begin to wither. Its leaves would fall off. Its branches and stem would become weak, and finally, the tree would shrivel and die.

What could cause such large and thriving trees to wither and die? When the trees were repeatedly abused and cursed, those words would gradually affect their vitality. As a result, they would lose their will to live and finally succumb to death.

Whether this story is true or not, it does convey an important message. It is quite possible that something similar might have happened to you or any of your acquaintances. Bearing the brunt of constant taunting and ridicule by people who would keep saying, "Why don't you just give up! You'll never be able to accomplish this."

Such demoralizing words are no less than curses. How badly would they have affected you? You wouldn't have continued working on that task for long and would have given up.

To cut a long story short, every negative word we use while addressing others badly affects them. It is the power of negative words propelled by negative feelings that forces even giant trees to shrivel and fall.

Take a minute to ponder: How often in a day do you hurl negative words at others or receive negative words from others? Many of us often don't have the slightest clue about how severely our words could be hurting others, perhaps even denting their morale and confidence permanently. We may not always mean what we say, but even these words uttered in ignorance can have a deeply demoralizing effect on the other person's subconscious mind. Our negative words, thoughts, and actions are like darts shot at others, which wound and scar them.

If our negative words can affect others negatively, then what about our positive words? Can they positively affect the other person? Of course, they can!

When someone sneezes, we habitually say "God bless you" to them. We also wish people "God bless you" on their birthday or when they bow to seek our blessings. By doing so, we purely wish for their wellbeing. "God bless you" symbolizes wishing well for others.

In this book, we are about to discover an exceptional power that we inherently possess. This power can work miraculously not only on us but also on others around us.

What is this exceptional power that we hold within us? What is this magic that energizes us over and over again? What is this force, which, when harnessed, can completely transform our lives?

It is the magical power of blessings that we often tend to take lightly!

When we wish well for others, our benevolent thoughts touch their lives in beautiful ways. Just as medicines cure physical wounds, blessings can heal mental wounds. Just as rays of light annihilate darkness, the unseen rays of blessings can annihilate negativity from someone's mind. The power of blessings works in unseen. In this book, we shall refer to these blessings as *rays*.

The literal meaning of the word "ray" is a thin beam of light. You might have seen a laser pen that shoots a fine beam that falls on any surface as a pointer of light. It is generally used to point at content projected on screens.

Doctors in the medical field use lasers to cure certain illnesses. Just as lasers, when pointed on someone, can diagnose their disease, and cure it, we too can radiate rays through our feelings, thoughts, and words to those around us! We can send out rays of positive thoughts and words to others, bringing about a magical transformation in their lives. In turn, we can also experience a transformation in our own life. We can witness our life taking a positive turn from being burdened with sorrow and worries to a life filled with love, joy, and peace.

If everyone starts sending rays of positive feelings and thoughts to one another, the wondrous transformation that can be brought about in everyone's life is beyond imagination! Most people have limited and constricted thinking due to which they cannot grasp the invisible laws of life. However, a seemingly simple ray of benevolence is potent to bring about miracles in our life.

We all would have observed that we often feel nice upon meeting certain people and uncomfortable meeting some others. Why does this happen? It's either because we think negatively about them, or they about us. As a result, both affect each other, and we feel negative.

Just as a blessed ray sent by us can create miracles in other's life, evil or negative rays can wreak havoc in the other person's life, provided they are receptive to it. Such is the astonishing power these seemingly simple rays have!

In the chapters that follow, we shall understand the power of these rays in depth. Let us learn to use them to benefit others and make our mind pure and holy in the process.

May all the positive powers of the universe help us in this endeavor! God bless and bliss us!

1
The Extraordinary Tree

There was an extraordinary tree that stood beside a beaten path on the outskirts of a village. There were many other trees, but this one was unique. Although it seemed just like any other tree, its uncommon characteristics made it very special.

Compared to the other trees, this tree would exhale double the amount of oxygen. Besides, it also had a compassionate heart that could perceive the emotions of people. But the tree was unaware of its unique qualities.

Many travelers to the town would take shelter under these trees to get over their fatigue before moving on. While resting under the other trees, the scorching rays of the afternoon sun would fall upon them. But when they rested under this tree, it would sense their discomfort and adjust its branches to shield them from the sweltering sunlight. The tree wasn't aware that this was a special ability that its neighboring trees lacked.

Every night, the tree would quietly express its heartfelt gratitude to God for being able to serve the travelers. It didn't have a clue about what was transpiring in the unseen realm because of this gratitude.

With time, the tree's relentless practice of helping and blessing everyone brought about an astounding change within it. It became even more capable and flexible. Now, it could sway its trunk to the left or right, thus serving travelers with even more affection and enthusiasm.

Slowly its capabilities grew to such an extent that the travelers resting under it could also sense it. They would exclaim, "There is something special about this tree. We feel so fresh and energetic." They would praise the tree from their heart, "What an extraordinary tree this is!"

When the travelers would rest under the tree, the tree would meditate and bring forth positive thoughts for them. Its positive vibrations would have a profound healing effect on them.

Some of them would be preoccupied with their problems when they would rest under the tree. They would think of going someplace, accomplishing certain tasks. They would be gripped by fears and worries. After resting under the tree, new ideas and solutions would emerge in their minds. This could happen because the positive vibrations radiated by the tree would help them shift their focus inward to the source of intuition within them.

For a few minutes, the travelers would dwell in this divine state of relaxed being, albeit unknowingly. As a result, their fatigue would disappear. They would feel refreshed and move on happy and satisfied. They could sense the uniqueness of the tree but couldn't nail down the reason behind it.

The tree would feel elated seeing their happy and contented faces. Considering its increased flexibility, the tree would wonder, "I couldn't do this earlier. How am I able to do it now?!"

Then a time came when the tree started walking to places where there were more travelers. It would stop when it would see someone approaching. People would rest under its shade. It would adjust itself to provide maximum comfort and blissfully immerse in meditation.

Before moving ahead with the story, let's understand its meaning. Some people often possess such extraordinary abilities that they are unaware of, just like the tree. The tree had dedicated itself to selfless service out of love and compassion.

Similarly, it is an extraordinary ability when we think positively for people, pray for them, and wish for their wellbeing. It is rare and difficult to attain. Although everyone inherently possesses this ability, few feel the urge to express it. In this book, we will learn about ways to express this extraordinary ability that lies hidden within each of us.

This extraordinary ability is associated with an extraordinary law that states, **"When you wish for the wellbeing of others out of sympathy, compassion, and selflessness, it helps in their upliftment and generates a surge of divine energy within you. If you are already blessed with this energy, then your level of awareness rises to the next level."**

The story of the extraordinary tree explains this law. When we send healing rays by way of sympathetic and compassionate feelings, thoughts, and words for others, we wish for their wellbeing, pray for them. Then those feelings not only bring about miraculous changes in their lives, but also fructify in our life in the form of blessings.

For example, when we send healing rays, "May you be showered with love and joy... May your life be filled with abundance... May you always be happy... May you be blessed with perfect health... May the divine grace shower on you forever... You are pure... You are part of divinity," then whatever we wish for others manifests in our life too. In short, when we wish, "God bless you" for others, "God *bliss* you" happens with us – we receive pure bliss in turn.

It is like the juicer that gets to taste the fruit juice first before it reaches others. The healing rays we send for others bring happiness in their lives, but they first work as blessings in our life. These blessings profoundly touch our life. Our state of being changes. Our mind becomes pure. We become more receptive to the highest aspects of creation.

Blessings bestowed by a pure mind fructify sooner. They render us enormous strength. They augment our mental and spiritual strength. They help us become complete in all aspects. When we start sending healing rays to others, when we bestow them with blessings, the great exceptional law starts functioning in our life.

Let's see what happened next with the extraordinary tree in the next chapter.

2
The Onset of Karmic Disease

We read the story of the extraordinary tree in the previous chapter. It was happy and contented in serving people out of compassion. Day by day, it became more capable and robust.

One day, a parrot flew in and perched on the tree. It had a red upper beak and a brown lower. So, we could call it Brownie. Brownie loved sitting on that tree. Soon it housed itself in the tree hollow and settled down comfortably. It would watch the travelers seated under the shade of the tree and keep chatting with the tree.

Brownie noticed that some travelers would have food and leave food crumbs behind. Some would scratch on the trunk of the tree with their nails. Children would twist and pluck its leaves. However, the tree ignored all of this. It benevolently arranged for their shade and blissfully showered love and blessings on them. It remained unaffected by their behavior.

Brownie was troubled by this. After holding back for many days, he finally spoke out, "What kind of a tree are you!? You serve people with utmost sincerity. You bear the scorching heat yourself the entire day and give them shelter and comfort. But what have you gained in return? Have they reciprocated your generosity? Have they ever thanked you even once? See how they simply set out on their way. Ungrateful people! Do they deserve your kindness and blessings?" The tree smiled back and ignored it.

Brownie kept consistently pecking and empoisoning the tree about the travelers. It became the main topic of its daily chat. It would observe the travelers' actions and leave no stone unturned to raise grievances about them.

"Oh, dear! Just look at what they're doing! They're wiping their dirty hands on your trunk and leaves. Look at that rowdy fellow! He's putting off his cigarette on you. Aren't you seeing them?"

The tree didn't pay any heed. However, Brownie also didn't leave a single opportunity for impressing its views upon the tree. It kept ranting, "My dear friend! Times have changed. It's the age of Tit-for-tat. That's the right thing to do. What's the outcome of all the good you've done for others? Are you even aware of what people say after taking shelter under you? Did you hear what they were discussing yesterday afternoon? They talked about building a boat, and they're thinking of cutting you down for the wood. My friend, if you don't wake up, these people will not let you live!"

Not a single day went by when Brownie didn't say something accusatory. Slowly, its daily chatter started affecting the tree. When one is constantly bombarded with the same poisonous words, something is bound to seep in. The tree began thinking differently; its attitude of service began to deteriorate. As it started getting convinced with the parrot's words, its purity of intent began to gradually subside. The abilities that it had grown over the years began to wane. Its flexibility began to disappear. Its ability to sense people's thoughts and feelings had weakened. It could feel rigidity and heaviness setting in. Finally, it lost its ability to move around and became stationary. The extraordinary tree had now descended to be an ordinary one. It could feel that something was amiss but couldn't place what exactly had gone wrong! It was disturbed by the sudden and seemingly inexplicable loss of its abilities.

The tree that was once brimming with bliss and gratitude was now visibly unhappy. The parrot would wander around and perch on the tree. It would ask the tree, "Why are you depressed? Whatever you're doing is justified. It's not wrong to resent those who are wrong." The tree would listen to the parrot but failed to understand that these very words of the parrot had triggered its rigidity.

So, what's the moral of the story? The parrot represents a particular facet of our mind, which can be called the "contrast" mind. The contrast mind is that facet of the mind which judges and compares everything and divides them into good-bad, black-white, rich-poor, fair-dark, etc. This facet of our mind makes our otherwise peaceful life troublesome. When we are trapped in the constant blabber of the contrast mind, we fail to break out of it despite our will. This is what happened with the tree too. It got overwhelmed by the parrot's incessant chatter and lost its happiness, peace, and relaxed state of being. Its purity vanished, and intellect became dull. This shunned it from higher possibilities in its life.

We, too, often get trapped in the contrast mind's futile chatter and focus on others' faults, weaknesses, and other negativities. We keep blaming them and complaining about them. In ignorance, we make use of such words that become a curse for them. We tend to easily tease people or put them down just for the sake of cheap entertainment. For example, we casually say words like, "He is mad," "She is stupid," "He is awful," "He doesn't know anything," etc.

We do not realize that every negative word said casually or seriously affects the other person, like a curse. These words block the highest possibilities in their life. They also generate dullness and impurity within us, which corrupts our deeds, and consequently, our energy level declines sharply.

One may wonder how the negative words or thoughts entertained by them for others can affect them. But that's the truth because the second part of the extraordinary law states –

Observing blemishes stains the purity of the observer. His energies diminish and higher possibilities of his life get blocked.

This means that when we observe blemishes in someone, when we describe it and think about it, the same negativity begins to thrive within us. Negative thoughts sap our energy.

Being unaware of this law, people keep focusing on others' weaknesses, shortcomings, and vices, and complain about them. Consequently, their negative feelings, thoughts, and words become a curse for others and cause great harm to themselves by breeding karmic disease within them. Karmic disease infests their karma, making them negative. It eats into their vitality and drains their energy, just like it happened with the tree.

The extraordinary tree was doing exceptionally well until the parrot started injecting it with the slow poison of negativity, thus giving rise to karmic disease within the tree.

Not many people are aware of this law; hence it can be called the "extraordinary" law. The laws of nature function ceaselessly in our lives, whether we know it or not.

Hence, we need to understand the extraordinary law and start reaping its benefits in our life. In various situations of life, we may encounter negativities in people, the contrast mind may provoke us to retaliate, but we should simply ignore it and continue with the service of showering rays of compassionate feelings, blessings, and prayers for others. This will help cure the karmic disease in others as well as us. In the process, our vitality and inner strength will be augmented.

Let us understand what happened to the tree in the next chapter.

3

Annihilation of Karmic Disease

The extraordinary tree started contemplating its deplorable state. It pondered about what had gone wrong that it had stopped making progress. It tried to understand what it was caught up with that was causing its decline.

A few days later, while the tree was in a deep state of contemplation, a saint came by and took his seat beneath the tree. The news about the great saint's arrival spread far and wide to the nearby villagers within no time. They started flocking to meet the saint to get an audience with him to pay respect and get solutions to their problems, for the saint was said to be a clairvoyant. The saint would spend the whole day patiently giving time to everyone who had come to meet him and address their problems. The tree was keenly listening to their conversations. All these days, it had only heard mundane conversations of travelers, but the wise words of the saint seemed out of the ordinary.

After all the visitors had left, the saint sat in meditation. When he got up, he bowed before the tree and thanked it in reverence. The tree was surprised as no one had ever thanked it before. It experienced some strength within. Encouraged by this feeling, it asked the saint for a solution to its problem. At the saint's request, the tree narrated all that had happened.

The saint smiled and asked, "Have you been listening to a parrot these days?" The tree was taken aback! *How does the saint know about the blabbering parrot?!* "Yes!" the tree exclaimed, "There's a parrot that keeps coming here very often."

The saint replied, "Henceforth, neglect whatever the parrot tells you. Ignore its words and, more importantly, stop mulling over them. Just continue performing your virtuous deeds; resume serving people with love and compassion. You are not aware, but your intent to serve people was your strength. That had empowered you to move around and walk to various places. Only one in a million trees gains the ability to move. The ability to walk around is even rarer! You are truly blessed to have this extraordinary ability; cherish it, nurture it!"

Having said this, the saint left. Now, the parrot would come, but the tree stopped paying attention to the parrot's words or responding to them. The parrot observed the perseveringly indifferent attitude of the tree and gradually stopped visiting the tree. The tree began getting back to its old feelings. Regardless of the way people behaved with it, it devoted its full attention to serving them to its fullest potential. It provided them shelter with love and compassion, and prayed for their wellbeing.

Slowly, it regained its flexibility. It could move and then walk around once again. It wholly dedicated itself to serving people. It rapidly started progressing as everything was now happening in awareness. Now, it was happier than before.

After few days, the saint revisited the tree. The tree thanked him profusely and said, "Thanks to your wise words! Now, I can move and walk once again. The joy that I am experiencing now is far more than what I used to experience earlier. There is nothing more left for me to achieve in life!"

The saint replied, "This is an excellent state! If you continue doing it, can you guess what will happen next? You will become a human being one day!"

The tree was awestruck by the saint's words. *How can a tree become a human being?!* It didn't sound logical!

"It has never happened in the history of trees. I've never heard about any such thing. How's it possible?" the tree asked.

The saint smiled, "I know that it's possible because I too was once a tree! The parrot used to visit me too. The contrast mind tried to poison my life, but eventually I could win over it. The parrot will keep coming. But you, too, should continue disregarding it and render the power of your benevolent attention to people. With pure intent, share your happiness and shelter with others. Continue praying for their wellbeing. Then one day, you too will become a human being, just like me!"

In this story, we discovered the highest possibility of the tree. But what does this story convey? What is *our* highest possibility as human beings? If human life can fall to the level of animal tendencies by indulging in hatred, anger, and ill-will, it can also rise to the exalted stature of Godliness. We will understand more about this in the subsequent chapters.

But we need not wait to start sending healing rays of compassion to people, bless them, and pray for their wellbeing so that the extraordinary law starts functioning in our lives.

The strength we will gain from this extraordinary and unique ability will destroy karmic disease and help us unlock our highest potential. We can also help others get rid of their karmic disease.

4

Understanding Karmic Disease

We know the importance of a balanced diet and regular exercises for keeping our body healthy. We vigorously work towards it. But what if someone suffers a disease and is unaware of it? Obviously, his disease will aggravate.

For example, a person is fond of relishing sweets, unaware that he has diabetes. He consumes sweets to his heart's content. Until he becomes aware of the disease, he doesn't get the thought of controlling his eating habit. He continues to indulge, and his illness becomes severe.

In the same way, while people are suffering from karmic disease, they are unaware of it. Modern medical science deals with physical ailments, whereas karmic disease is related to our karma. Due to lack of awareness of its existence, we never think of getting rid of it. Let us understand what this disease is, how it corrupts our karma and worsens the quality of our life.

When our feelings, thoughts, speech, or behavior become negative, we get infected by karmic disease. When we think negatively about someone, curse them, wish them ill or hate them, such karma gives rise to karmic disease.

Usually, we consider our external actions as karma. Hence, so long as we do not act negatively in the world, we don't feel that we are promoting karmic disease. The truth is that karma is not only restricted to visible action, but also comprises the intent and feeling behind the action, the thoughts that are harbored while performing the action, and the words spoken about it. The quality of our karma is determined by all these four aspects.

For example, a dacoit and a surgeon both use a knife. But their karmas are so different. The dacoit uses the knife to threaten and kill people, whereas the surgeon uses it to save lives. They both use nearly the same tool, but their intentions are a world apart.

Karma backed by negative intentions indicates the presence of karmic disease. Moreover, such corrupt karma aggravates the disease.

When we feel hateful, envious, or angry about someone, or refer to them as insane, backbite them, or engage in negative gossip or spread bad rumors about them, we should realize that we're afflicted by karmic disease. Such karma binds us in karmic bondage and intensifies the disease. The symptoms of this disease are so subtle that we fail to recognize them.

In most situations, we lack full awareness of our feelings, thoughts, and negative words. Even in the most insignificant situation, we may utter some words carelessly out of habit. Let's understand this with the help of an example.

Imagine you're driving on the road, and a car speedily overtakes you. He drives away so rashly that you can't help but hold your breath. You instinctively yell at him, "Are you crazy? Go, kill yourself if you wish, but why do you want to kill others along with you?! You will learn only when you meet with an accident!"

If someone does something unpleasant to us, our mind immediately starts its chatter. Not for a single moment do we ponder from the other's point of view. "Why did he drive so fast? Why was he in such a hurry? Was he in an emergency?" Instead, we immediately consider the person wrong and hurl curses at him.

The words we utter in anger are nothing but curses that touch the person, however far he goes past us. While we curse explicitly using words in some situations, in some other situations we silently sulk within and indulge in incessant negative thoughts like blame.

A homemaker asks each of her family members what they would like to have for dinner. Then she gets to making dishes based on their preferences. Now, outwardly this may seem to be good karma, but what about her thoughts? While making dinner, what if she is thinking, "Everyone just places their order and sits back like a lord. Am I their maid to be constantly at their beck and call? Now I need to clean the utensils too. No one bothers to help me."

In this example, ourwordly her karma appears good, but her negative feelings give rise to karmic disease. Her negative feelings and thoughts not only corrupt the quality of her karma but also badly affect the food and those who consume it, though it may not be felt tangibly. Thus, even if the karma appears good externally, it still breeds karmic disease if the underlying feelings and intent are negative.

Our words and actions are visible outside, but no one can fathom our feelings or thoughts. Hence, the resultant karma is also hidden. If no one ever pinpoints our mistakes or guides us by imparting higher understanding, we will continue to dwell in negative feelings and thoughts. This further contaminates our karma and aggravates the karmic disease.

Most often, one fails to understand why they perform such karma much against their will. Karmic disease is the culprit behind it. Having understood what karmic disease is, let us understand the reasons behind the disease in the next chapter.

5
Causes of Karmic Disease

Many people have heard of the Law of Karma, which states– what goes around, comes around. Whatever deeds we perform, the way we behave with others, return to us at some time or the other. Despite knowing this, we continue to act in ways that wrongly backfire on us.

We entertain negative feelings and thoughts for others and hurt them through our words due to karmic disease. Karmic disease can have various causes. Let us now understand them.

1. Upbringing

The way we have been brought up and the negative incidents we have been through in our life have played an influential role in causing karmic disease within us. Our upbringing influences our perception and behavior.

For example, some people feel rejected by their family. This especially happens in families with two or more siblings—one is good at academics and sport, and the other isn't. The former receives all the love, affection, and appreciation from parents and other family members. He or she gets rewarded for an excellent performance. In contrast, the latter is invariably at the receiving end of criticism, comparison, advice, and taunts. However hard he or she tries, people keep pointing their shortcomings; being appreciated is far-fetched.

Slowly, the latter one cringes and shrinks within. He starts considering himself inferior, and a deep feeling of rejection takes root. This negative emotion then takes the form of karmic disease. Even after growing up, he has difficulty in expressing his thoughts, ideas, or feelings for fear of rejection. This constricted feeling doesn't let him function to the fullest of his potential.

Some children are subject to traumatic incidents where they feel helpless. They quietly bear through the trauma, without defending themselves or retaliating. Due to a suppressed rage, they grow up to be angry adults. The smallest of setbacks or disagreements trigger their anger. They feel irritated all the time with something or the other and keep seething within. The suppressed emotions from their childhood have taken the form of karmic disease. It contaminates their present karma.

2. Tendencies

Tendencies are deep-rooted habits and inclinations. First, man makes habits, and then habits make man. Tendencies compel us to act according to our old set patterns. This is an indication that tendencies have taken the form of karmic disease.

If a drunkard or a smoker is asked, "Do you think what you're doing is right?" what would he say? If he is honest, he will testify, "Not at all! This habit is badly affecting my health. It's spoiling my relationships. I'm also wasting money on it. I want to break free of this habit but am unable to."

The person knows how harmful the habit is, and yet he is helpless due to his tendencies. Satisfying his urges becomes an involuntary compulsion.

Every obese person very well knows the importance of regular exercises and a healthy dietary regime for his fitness. If he ignores them, he will be in for a health disorder. Yet, he fails to take corrective action and indulges in unhealthy food habits and skips exercises.

In the same way, people know that expressing anger causes them the most harm. It disturbs harmony in their relationships and adversely affects their health. Yet, they become angry if things don't turn the way they wish.

These examples demonstrate how tendencies drive us to act in ways much against our will. They compel us to indulge in our old, ingrained habits. These tendencies take the form of karmic disease and corrupt our karma.

3. Core thoughts

A core thought is a firm belief that is ingrained in our mind since our childhood. For example, some people strongly believe, "Money is at the root of all evil" or "I get money but can't hold onto it for long." These core thoughts drive us to engage in deeds that don't let us hold onto money for long or have strained relationships with people on money matters.

Some strongly believe that this is not the era for doing good for others. They are convinced that honesty does not pay in this world. These thoughts affect their karma. They adopt the path of lies and deceit. Shrewdness and cunning become their second nature. As a result, they remain bereft of doing good for others.

These core thoughts are so strong and deeply rooted in their minds that they get proofs of their validity, which in turn reinforce these beliefs further. This happens according to the law of nature – **That which you strongly believe in, manifests in your reality.**

If someone believes, "The world is full of bad people," then he is bound to encounter only bad people in his life. His wrong belief becomes a reality for him.

In this way, the dominant deep-rooted thoughts that dwell within us since childhood shape our life. Positive core thoughts help us grow in life, whereas negative core thoughts create karmic disease.

4. Injured memories

Injured memories are unhealed, hurtful memories that are a result of an ordeal we have been through. There are two types of injured memories: those that come from our own experiences, and those placed within us or inherited by us when we were born.

The first kind is easy to understand. These injured memories come from our own experiences during our lifetime. These memories are so deeply entrenched that we repeatedly experience their impact on our life. Until they are healed, they keep troubling us time and again. Despite our will, we can't get rid of them. They drive our behavior and actions. Let's understand this with an example.

Karan and Vishal were school friends. Once, they had a dispute in their class. The teacher punished Karan but let Vishal free. Karan couldn't take this insult. He developed grudges against Vishal. He formed a firm belief that the teacher let Vishal free because of his family's wealthy status. He felt angry about the injustice meted out to him. He developed jealousy for Vishal's wealth and social status. This childhood incident became an injured memory for him. Whenever he would see wealthy people having an easy life, the wound caused by the injured memory would get triggered, and he would relive the same hurtful feelings again and again.

The second kind of injured memories is subtler. Physical bodies perish with time, but injured memories don't. After the death of that body, nature transfers these injured memories into other newborn bodies to heal them. Until they are healed completely, nature continues transferring them into new bodies. Thus, every human being is born with some injured memories.

It is due to this reason that we experience a Deja vu at times. We visit some place and feel, "I have been here before," even though we would have never been there before. We get a deep feeling that we have been through certain situations before, whereas we can't recollect them. This happens due to injured memories.

If we don't pay proper attention to our physical wounds, they don't heal. Gradually, they aggravate and infect other parts of our body. The same happens with mental wounds too. An injured memory is like a wound at a psychic level that needs to be treated and healed in time. But since no one knows about it, they never get the thought of healing them. Consequently, they take the form of a karmic disease and affect our present actions.

5. Beliefs

Our contrast mind is like an incessant chatterbox. We blindly believe whatever it says and logically reason based on it. Considering our logical conclusion to be true, we formulate our own stories around it. Conditioned by our childhood memories and influenced by the beliefs of our parents, teachers, friends, and neighbors, we reinforce these beliefs. We are firmly convinced that whatever we have believed is the ultimate and unequivocal truth.

Consider a child who has grown up hearing his elders say, "Our religion is the supreme and the most perfect among all religions." Its constant repetition makes him believe, "Yes, this is the ultimate truth." The truth is that all religions preach the same teachings. They teach us the virtues of brotherhood, love, goodwill, compassion, and kindness. However, the child's beliefs stop him from believing in this universal truth. Ultimately, these beliefs breed karmic disease within him.

For some people, various incidents in their life become the cause of their karmic disease. Some inherit karmic disease from their parents through their genes. Consequently, they feel suffocated and suffer from stress, fear, insecurity, and other defilements. Sometimes, even doctors fail to diagnose the cause of their ailments as the cause lies in their karmic disease, which is invisible.

In conclusion, whatever be the causes of the karmic disease, the consequences have grave effects on our life. We will understand the consequences of karmic disease in the next chapter.

6

The Effects of Karmic Disease

People often tend to mete out the same feelings that they receive from others. If others talk to them with love and compassion, they respond likewise. If others mete out anger, hatred, or jealousy at them, they too reciprocate in the same manner. People often get influenced by vengeful feelings and retaliate in the same measure. This reflex behavior aggravates karmic disease on a mass scale to such an extent that it enshrouds the entire world in its web.

People are unaware of the role of karmic disease in the difficulties they face in their life. It is high time that everyone becomes aware of this invisible disease so that they can take steps to cure it and save not only themselves but also those around them. Let us look at how karmic disease affects us and understand its harmful effects.

1. Negative thoughts

Karmic disease affects our thinking first. All the negative feelings, thoughts, and words we harbor for others degrades our perspective.

We become so negatively programmed that we see only negatives in people and situations around us.

Such negative thinking raises our stress and affects our actions. We wonder, "Why do I mentally feel so heavy and loaded these days?" When we fail to nail down the root cause, we blame it on people and situations. "My boss is causing me all the stress," "I wish I had better friends," "I am unable to live comfortably because of my spouse," "I have the most non-cooperative siblings ever," and so on. The more we hold others responsible for our stress, we get increasingly trapped in the downward spiral of complaints and accusations.

2. Obstructing free flow

A river naturally flows freely. When its free flow is obstructed, the water becomes stagnant, and this stagnancy can even become toxic. Similarly, when we are in the feeling of free-flow, all our tasks—whether in the office or at home—happen spontaneously and effortlessly in a natural flow. We feel pleasant and attuned to nature all the time.

However, as karmic disease increases, it obstructs this feeling of free flow. Initially, the feeling dims and then gradually vanishes. Then the same tasks that were happening smoothly begin to feel like a burden; accomplishing them becomes a great ordeal.

3. Weakening of spiritual strength and contamination of the aura

All of us have an aura that radiates from our inner being. It is an energy field surrounding our physical body. It is at its peak during our childhood. Anyone encountering a child experiences its strong aura even from a far distance. Hence, everyone loves being in its company.

However, as we grow up, our mind gets trapped in the mire of negative feelings leading to karmic disease. This, in turn, weakens our aura and diminishes our spiritual strength.

4. Sowing the seeds of violence

When parents are inflicted by karmic disease, they unknowingly abuse and accuse their children. The reasons could be the child's failure, mischiefs, or the parents being already irritated with something. Due to karmic disease, they cannot tolerate the simple mistakes or mischiefs of their children. Instead, they severely punish their children, expecting the punishment will set their children straight.

When children sense that their family does not accept them, they look out for such friends who accept and approve them. Often these friends, by themselves, are unfortunately lost and misguided. They use such children to their own benefit. Slowly, these children grow into adults inclined towards violence and anti-social behavior, indulging in immoral activities. Thus, the seeds of violence thrive in such children in their early childhood. Hence, many of them even don't shy away from using destructive weapons.

Thus, karmic disease affects us not just in trivial ways but also at a very deep and far-reaching scale. As a result, we get trapped in a multitude of problems.

To safeguard ourselves from the harmful effects of karmic disease and eliminate them completely, we need to conquer the negativity within us and spread positivity around us. We need to learn the art of converting the curses arising from our negative feelings, thoughts, and words into compassionate rays of blessings. Showering such compassionate rays of wellbeing on others alone can destroy the karmic disease that has spread worldwide.

In the following chapters, we will understand what these rays are, and how and on whom these rays should be showered.

7

The Meaning of Healing Rays

"You are perfect in your own way. Don't consider yourself wrong. Forget all that has happened and take action that is appropriate for this moment. You are capable. You have immense potential."

When you find yourself in challenging situations where people test your patience, does it occur to you to bless them with such compassionate words? If you do, then you are heading in the right direction as these are not mere words but potent blessings. These words of compassion and encouragement hold the potential to heal and uplift not just the recipients but also the giver. This is the magic of healing rays.

Let us understand what healing rays are in detail.

The word "ray" commonly refers to a thin beam of light. However, in the context of this book, "ray" refers to **radiating goodwill and** wellbeing to others, spreading positivity through our feelings, thoughts, words, and actions.

The purpose of showering healing rays is to free one from their karmic disease, from karmic bondage. Every feeling, thought, and word emanating from our pure loving presence holds extraordinarily immense power. It can heal people and bring a positive outcome to challenging situations. Even one glance at people with the eye of compassion can uplift them, provided it arises from the bedrock of faith.

When faith peeks out through our eyes, when our heart is filled with benevolence, and speech is enriched with positive words, we not only live our own life happily, gracefully, and peacefully but also help others live the same way. To gain such power, let us understand the various dimensions of healing rays.

1. Looking with the eye of healing

If any of your relatives, neighbors, or friends are unwell and admitted to a hospital, how do you see them? Do you see them with the eye of healing? Or do you watch them pitifully and hopelessly, thinking, "Poor fellow! How sick and weak he's become! This is awful! He does not deserve such hardships"?

Most people wish to help the sick and unwell. But they perceive these people as helpless and hopeless. Their perception transmits their negative energy to the sick. This further drains the sick of their energy and pushes them deeper into their affliction. Thus, despite wanting to help, they fail to help the sick.

When we perceive the sick with the eye of healing, we help them heal faster. When we entertain positive thoughts for them, like, "Don't worry, you will be up and about soon! You're already becoming healthy. You're blessed with divine healing," such feelings, thoughts, and words energize him and promote healing. By doing this, we send healing rays to him.

2. Blessings others

In the olden days, when soldiers used to set out to battle, they would seek blessings from their elders as the first thing. They knew the power of blessings and had faith that the elders' blessings would come to fruition for sure. Even today, in many cultures around the world, when someone sets out to accomplish some auspicious work, he is advised to seek blessings from his elders so that his work can be completed.

Some of the blessings that are bestowed are: "May God bless you! May all your work be completed successfully! May all your wishes come true! May you attain success in all your endeavors! Your success is assured! May you return victorious! Wish you well!"

Blessing people is a positive act of selflessness. By doing this, we send positive energizing rays to people to help them in their times of distress.

3. Praying and wishing well for others

Best wishes play an important role in our life. When we wish well for others, they get energized with a positive feeling. They feel good that at least someone is thinking good for them. When we give best wishes to a student appearing for his exams, he feels optimistic. When we wish "Get well soon" to someone admitted to a hospital, he feels happy that someone cares for him and wants him to be cured. When someone sneezes, we say, "God bless you!" These are examples where we wish well for others and shower healing rays on them.

When we selflessly pray for others, we shower healing rays. Just as the machine that extracts juice from the sugarcane is the first one to taste it, people sending healing rays to others are themselves benefitted before anyone else. It is unimaginable how the prayers we perform for others bring miracles in our own life! Hence, continue sending healing rays through prayers.

4. Being in gratitude

Gratitude, by itself, is not just a quality but a way of life. Instead of brooding over what we don't have, when we express gratitude for what we have, we shift from a perspective of lacking to that of having, from scarcity to abundance.

When someone helps us or guides us on time, we immediately express gratitude for that person, wish well for him. At that time, we don't realize that we have showered healing rays on him in the unseen by expressing heartfelt gratitude. They will bring miraculous positive results in our life as well. The feeling of gratitude also raises our own inner purity. Hence, we should always stay in a perpetual feeling of gratitude – both for the people around us and for nature.

5. Always having positive thoughts

We are constantly engaged in self-talk in our mind. They could be positive or negative thoughts about ourselves or others. Most of the time, we are unaware that each thought that we entertain is bound to affect our life or someone else's. Our every positive thought—about ourselves or others—is like a healing ray. Hence, always inculcate only positive thoughts. Bear in mind that our one positive thought has the potential to change our life as well as that of others.

6. Forgiving and seeking forgiveness

Throughout the day, in various situations, we may be hurting people through our feelings, thoughts, speech, and action, knowingly or unknowingly. This results in the formation of karmic bondage with them, which further intensifies the karmic disease. Hence, whenever this happens, immediately seek forgiveness from them to get free from the karmic bondage. If not verbally, make sure that you do it in your mind at the least. This helps weaken the karmic disease.

It is an unseen law of nature that our thoughts and feelings reach out to people. When we think or feel negatively about someone, those thoughts and feelings reach out to that person. As soon as we seek forgiveness from them, even those feelings reach out to them and help heal their hurtful wounds. Thus, seeking forgiveness or forgiving someone is like showering healing rays that help heal the wounds of the other person.

When we see dirt in our home, we immediately clean it. We do not keep it for later, for the longer we wait, the dirtier our home can get. Likewise, as soon as any negative feeling, thought, word or action arises within us, we need to immediately wipe it off with the duster of forgiveness. This saves not only us but also others from the aggravation of karmic disease.

Karmic disease increases with every trivial or major incident. We can see the intensity and collective quantum of karmic disease in the whole world, and yet we see that the world is moving on! This is because while a lot of people end up creating karmic disease due to their negative contribution, an increasing number of people shower healing rays by practicing forgiveness. They understand the importance of forgiving and letting go. Hence, they help maintain balance in the world by seeking forgiveness and forgiving others.

"Let God forgive you, let God forgive me, let God forgive all, you also please forgive me." One can heal the karmic disease by uttering such healing lines. The practice of forgiveness is the best tool to eliminate impure thoughts and instill healing rays in their place.

Just as sunrays help in curing humans and trees of various diseases, positive healing rays cure the entire world of its diseases. They eradicate all ill feelings from our mind. Hence, continue sending healing rays through your feelings, thoughts, and words.

In the next chapter, we shall see how healing rays work in our lives.

8
The Science of Healing Rays

To understand how healing rays affect others, let us understand the science behind it. When we pray positively for someone, when we bless them, we actually transmit healing rays towards them. These healing rays are positive, compassionate, health-giving, healing vibrations. They positively affect our physical health as well as all aspects of our life in turn. Although they function in the unseen, their effect is certain.

Just like a positive, compassionate vibration is sent to the other person when we pray for them, a negative, hurtful vibration is sent when we curse them. While positive vibrations help destroy our own karmic disease besides others', negative vibrations intensify it further for everyone.

In the modern scientific age, a lot of scientific research has been carried out to study the effect of vibrations from blessings and curses. In an experiment with water, scientists filled three glasses of water from the same source. The water in the first glass was blessed and thanked. The water in the second glass was left as it is without saying anything. The water in the third glass was cursed with negative words like, "Dirty water, bad water, stinking water." This practice was repeated for a few days.

Then the water in each glass was crystallized and observed under a microscope. Crystals of water in the first glass that was blessed and thanked formed brilliant, well-formed, symmetrical patterns. Crystals of water in the second glass that was not exposed to anything were quite regular. Whereas crystals of the water in the third glass subjected to curses formed incomplete, asymmetric, chaotic patterns.

This startling discovery demonstrates the extent of impact vibrations can have on our body and mind. More than 60% of the human body is water. When we harbor negative feelings for others, when we curse others, it affects us first. Our body and mind get contaminated, intensifying our karmic disease. It also affects others negatively. On the other hand, when we are full of positive, benevolent feelings and send blessings, healing rays to others, our mind becomes pure, and body becomes healthy.

With the understanding that the science of vibrations works on everything, it becomes imperative for us to send only vibrations arising out of positive words and use them to the benefit of all beings; to spread health, love, joy, and peace in the entire world. Even a few people can start this revolution by sending healing rays; the positivity will spread to every corner of the world.

When the plants in our garden get infected, we use disinfectants and fertilizers to save them. We place them in such a way that they receive enough sunlight. Thus, solar therapy cures them of their infection. In the same way, we also need to radiate benevolent feelings through healing rays to destroy karmic disease and free ourselves and others from the defilements of anger, hatred, jealousy, ill-will, and guilt.

Sending vibrations of benevolent feelings is the best tool to heal our thoughts and cure the karmic disease within us. This triggers healing within us at the mental and physical level.

Thus, having understood how we can cure our karmic disease, we must also take a step further and understand how we can avoid creating this disease in the first place. All we need is faith and awareness. When faith awakens, before saying or thinking negatively about anyone, we will carefully consider whether it will lead to karmic disease or healing. Then we will consciously choose only healing rays. With consistent practice, our nature will gradually become completely positive. We will think and speak only positive words that will radiate benevolent feelings in and through all life situations. This will help us align with the divine will. When we start fulfilling the divine will, we begin showering the rays of benevolent feelings everywhere.

We need an increasing number of benevolent thinkers today to eradicate the effect of karmic disease from the world and spread the magic of healing rays everywhere. Our sole contribution is to always shower ourselves and others with divine healing rays. This can eventually help annihilate everything that has happened in the past and create a bright future for mankind.

9

The Effect of Positive Words

In the earlier chapter, we have seen how blessings help shower healing rays on others. In the Indian culture, when someone sets out for an auspicious work, they take blessings from the elders. In Western culture, before undertaking something important, they are wished, "Good luck!" "God Bless You!"

These practices are not a mere formality. They were designed with the specific aim of getting people to bless each other and send healing rays. When these prayers and blessings are genuinely evoked from the bottom of the heart, they bear miraculous results.

When we say positive words for someone, they indeed affect the other person positively, but they first benefit us. We become pure from within. Our karmic disease weakens. When we utter words backed by feelings, the feelings and vibrations together positively affect us as well as the other person.

Words have amazing power. You may have read books or seen films about the stories of saints and sages. When they would become angry, they would curse. When they would be pleased with the devotion and surrender of the seeker, they would grant boons to them. Every word they spoke, whether good or bad, came true.

But in the modern era, when someone blesses or curses someone, why doesn't it bear fruit?

Whether they are boon or curse, the words spoken won't come to fruition unless they are backed by spiritual strength and uttered from the bottom of the heart with purity of mind. The saints and sages led an ascetic life. Their steadfast and rigorous spiritual practice helped raise the purity of their body and mind. The words they spoke, the emotions they felt, emanated from this purity. Their words were energized by the purity of their mind, their selflessness, and their spiritual strength. Hence, every word they spoke was as good as a prophecy. Further, their disciples also had implicit faith that it had to manifest if their master had said something.

However, when our minds are filled with hatred, jealousy, anger, dishonesty, and deceit in the present era, it is worth considering how much power our positive words can have.

The fact is that our words don't possess the power that saints and sages had. We waste our power by engaging in criticism, exaggeration, deceit, and dishonesty. We don't trust what we say. Our feelings, thoughts, speech, and action are not in rhythm with one another. Hence, there is a big difference in what we say, what we think, what we feel, and what we do.

But we need not lose hope. We can surely attain purity of body and mind, and spiritual strength to energize our words. The practice of meditation, rendering selfless service, identifying our negative behavior patterns and working on them, chanting mantras, and practice of yoga can help us in this endeavor. They cleanse us of the negativity within us and fill us with positive energy. The healing rays we send to others with such purity and positivity will have a definite effect.

In fact, sending healing rays to others should become our second nature. In situations where we are unable to send lengthy sentences as healing rays, we may as well say, "God bless you!" "Thank you!" or "Wish you best!" They work like a mantra. We can use them in any situation. We can also write them on our mobile as a reminder. Gradually, we will get attuned with such words to such an extent that we will start sending healing rays effortlessly by using them.

How can we send healing rays when their effect is not seen immediately?

Sometimes, we may not be able to see the visible effects of healing rays immediately. This is because the other person may not be receptive to our prayers. He may be overwhelmed with pain, or he may not be willing to recover, or he may be so constricted that he has blocked his receptivity and is unable to trust anyone. How can we send healing rays in such cases?

In such cases, we should not say any positive, healing sentences to them directly because their conscious mind will reject them outright. Instead, we should communicate with their subconscious mind at night when it is fully receptive. When they are in a deep sleep at night, we can send healing rays from a state of absolute purity to their subconscious mind. The subconscious mind will then work upon our healing prayers and bring about changes in their life. They won't even realize that it is the effect of someone's prayers in their life. Bless them with words like:

"You are pure; You are purity.

You will attain everything that is right for you

as per your Divine Plan, your desire, or even better than that.

You are surrounded by people of higher consciousness

who are helping you attain your purpose on Earth

to reach the highest evolved state.

Let there be harmony in your relationships.

May you attain the best health."

We need to mentally project such powerful blessings to the other person's subconscious mind. This will gradually bring about remarkable holistic changes in their life, benefitting not only them but also those around them. This will help free them from their karmic disease. Such healing rays emanating from our heart will also heal and free us from our karmic disease. We will also receive blessings in turn. In this way, we will become instrumental in curing karmic disease of others. Start sending healing rays selflessly, and as per the extraordinary law, our highest potential will unleash on its own. We will attain the highest evolved state of being.

Even in the present era, this is possible provided people work upon their minds and wish well for others. We can start practicing this from our homes. While leaving home, seek blessings from elders, bless the young, send healing rays to those who are of our age so that everyone receives blessings and positivity.

10

Whom Should We Send Healing Rays?

Our life is shaped by the karma we perform through our feelings, thoughts, words, and actions. Positive karma brings about peace and happiness in our life, whereas negative karma intensifies our karmic disease. We cannot stop performing karma. But if we have performed negative karma, we can send healing rays to annihilate the resultant karmic disease. Healing rays help us become free of all bondage that holds us back from realizing our true potential.

Now, let us understand whom we should send healing rays and how we can experience freedom in our life.

1. Send healing rays to yourself first

When we are happy, we wish to share the experience of happiness with others. However, when we are unhappy, we feel that the entire world is grief-stricken. In such a state, we are unable to think good for others. An unhappy mind shuts itself up and is hence incapable of blessing others and wishing them well. Therefore, we must first help ourselves; we must rise above the need for help before we can help others.

Only when we are healthy, we understand the importance of being healthy and wish that others also experience the healthy feeling. Similarly, to share happiness with others and send them healing rays, we need to first experience the happiness that we would feel by helping them. We need to bask in that feeling and sustain it. For that, we must first work upon ourselves to eradicate the karmic disease formed due to our negative feelings and thoughts. We must begin praying for ourselves. Bless, love, and send healing rays to ourselves so that our mind opens to positivity again.

We can express our love and care for our body by keeping it healthy. Gently caress it, touch each body part, and thank it, "Thank you for your best support. Be always healthy!" Whenever we remember, we should bless our body, "God bless you, my dear body! I love you!"

Whenever we remember, we should bless ourselves, "I am pure. I am the darling of God." Blessing ourselves with such benevolent feelings helps us tide through difficult situations where negative feeling arises.

Let us understand this with some examples.

Consider you need to walk into an interview. But your mind is nervous, worrying, "What will the interviewers ask me? Will I be able to answer them? Will I get the job?" and so on. At such times, start sending healing rays to yourself by repeating, "I am capable. I am complete. I am competent. Everything is possible for me." Soon, you will feel more confident and relaxed.

Sending healing rays to ourselves in this manner can pull us out of the quagmire of negativity and fill us with positive, rejuvenating energy in any situation. This helps us come out of that situation comfortably.

Sometimes, we feel guilty or remorseful over a fight or an argument with someone. We keep lingering over it for a long time and regret it. We can break free from this state by sending healing rays to ourselves. We can tell ourselves, "Whatever has happened, happened for good. It's not a big deal. Now, you surrender unto the divine healing light. You're not wrong. The situation makes it seem wrong. You are pure. You are sacred. You are an inseparable part of divinity." We can use any other positive words as well to send healing rays to ourselves.

2. Send healing rays to others

We all, knowingly or unknowingly, are constantly engaged in some form of karma. Karma does not necessarily mean tangible actions. They can be our feelings, thoughts, and spoken words too – whether negative or positive. Negative karma results in karmic bondage with others.

After performing any negative karma, even in our feelings or thoughts, we should immediately seek forgiveness from the other person, if not verbally then at least mentally. Then we should send healing rays to ourselves and the other person so that both can be free from the karmic bondage. We can say, "I am pure and sacred. You, too, are pure and sacred. Let God bestow both of us with the right wisdom." We will immediately feel relieved after that.

In this way, we can send healing rays using such chosen words to others in their challenging situations and help them come out of those situations.

3. Send healing rays to inert objects

We use many objects during our daily life. They make our life easy. Yet, we never thank them for their service. We handle them carelessly, throw them around. Sometimes, we knowingly or unknowingly use wrong words for these objects out of frustration. And yet, they constantly serve us.

With frequent use, these objects could go out of order for various reasons. At such times, instead of getting frustrated, we should send them healing rays so that they resume functioning. This may sound illogical, but be assured it works. If you find it hard to believe, experiment with it.

If your mobile phone stops working intermittently, start sending healing rays to it. Gently hold it in your hand and lovingly caress it. Then say, "You work for me relentlessly every day, but I have never thanked you. Thank you for your service! Please forgive me for not caring enough for you. You are fantastic and efficient! You are more than capable of working for long hours. My benevolent feelings and best wishes are always with you. You can heal yourself. Thank you for healing yourself!"

We can also send healing rays to objects that we have misplaced and are unable to find. After some time, we will see that we will either remember where they are kept or come across them when we are least expecting them.

4. Send healing rays to food and water

Sending healing rays to food and water a minute before consuming them can do wonders for our health. It has been scientifically proven that food and water can be purified through prayer.

Sending healing rays to food energizes it with positive energy. Such food makes our mind and body pure and healthy. Before serving food, bless it with healing rays so that it becomes tasty and renders health for those who consume it. We can also send healing rays to the food as we prepare it, "I bless this food. May all those who consume it be blessed with good health and a positive mind!"

We have understood how healing rays can bring about transformation in our life through many examples. Healing rays can be sent to people, objects, food, and water. They bring about positive changes in all of them. Although they may appear to be small statements, considering their effect, you ought to make them a part of your life.

11

Who Needs Healing Rays the Most?

As most people are unaware of the potential of healing rays, they unknowingly create karmic disease through their karma and aggravate it. When one curses the other person, unknown to him, the karmic disease spreads in the environment, radiating negativity all around. People begin to feel hatred and compulsively curse one another, thereby deteriorating their quality of life even further. So, it is essential that everyone learns to send healing rays so that all beings on Earth are healed and their lives improve.

We have seen that our life is affected by both – karmic disease and healing rays – but their impact is entirely different. While karmic disease inflicts us and others when we curse them through our feelings, thoughts, or speech, healing rays act as an agent to reduce and nullify the effects of this karmic disease.

To send healing rays, let us now understand who needs these rays the most. To answer this, ask yourself, how many people would be remembering you right now.

While leading a worldly life, we are enmeshed with so many people. They could be our family, friends in school or college, colleagues at the workplace, neighbors, the government, civic authorities, etc. But how many of them would be remembering us at this moment?

Some would say two, some would say five or more, and it would be ten or more for some others. One may say that at least one person is surely remembering him. Each one's answer may differ. What is your answer? How many people would be remembering you right now? Take a pause and reflect on this.

Now, contemplate the next question: Why are they remembering you?

Someone may remember you because they've had a conflict with you or have perhaps loaned you money. Someone else may be remembering you for a task that they want you to do. Some may not be consciously remembering you right now, but they have some tasks that are pending for you to reach them at the earliest. Some people could even be remembering you in their attempt to forget you! And some could be remembering you out of love and affection. Thus, some people are remembering you with positive feelings and some with negative feelings.

Now, reflect: How many of them could be feeling better or worse after remembering you? How do people feel after remembering you?

Also, consider those people whom *you* are remembering. How do you feel about them when you remember them? This is very important because our feelings are the medium through which either healing rays or curses are sent forth. As this happens in the unseen, we are unaware of it. As a result, we either send healing rays or create karmic disease for one another.

The next important question is: Of all the people who are remembering you, which are the ones who need healing and good health? Who needs blessings to make them feel good? Do the ones who feel better after remembering you need healing? Or do the ones who feel worse after remembering you need healing? Who needs it more? Those who connect positively with you, or those who connect with a negative feeling?

It is very important to understand the answer to this question. Logically, one may think, "Why should we bless those who harbor negative feelings for me? I won't care for them and can afford to hate them."

It seems justified to admire and bless those who remember us with positive feelings. However, the converse is true. Those who experience troubled feelings, harbor contempt, feel scared or rejected after remembering you deserve your blessings and healing rays because they need it the most!

We know very well that the sick need to be treated, not the healthy. Doctors prescribe medication for the sick. In the same way, healing is required the most for those who feel low, whose mind is inflicted with hatred, malice, and envy. But usually, people bless those who do noble work and curse those who engage in sinful deeds.

Ironically, those who connect with us negatively and need our blessings and healing do not receive them. They receive just the opposite, the result of which is disastrous. The terrorists of today should have been accepted by their families and neighbors when they had committed small mistakes as children. But many of them are rejected and scorned during their childhood. As a result, they go astray as they grow up and turn to wrong ways.

Thus, be it on a small scale or a large, even a little curse can lead to a significant outcome. And it can be healed with a little blessing too! Now, you need to reflect on what you have been sending to people so far and choose what you will send hereafter. This conscious choice is most important.

Some people are rendering the noble service of sending healing rays to others, thereby helping in fostering and maintaining harmony in the world. But when increasingly many people gain this understanding about healing rays and join in this mission, when all the needy ones receive healing rays, then not only trivial problems but even major issues like terrorism that ail the world can be resolved.

Let us understand this in depth with one more example. When someone scolds another in front of you, whom do you sympathize with—the one who scolds or the one who is scolded?

Usually, in such a scenario, the onlookers sympathize more with the one who is *being* scolded. They feel compassion for the victim and become angry and displeased with the perpetrator. This is but natural because, at that moment, the one who is at the receiving end of the scolding appears pitiable, and the one who scolds appears merciless. Hence, they spontaneously curse the one who is scolding. However, they don't realize that they are intensifying the perpetrator's karmic disease by doing so. That person who is compulsively reacting with anger, doesn't deserve curses but blessings; he needs to be forgiven.

If we go deeper and analyze the root cause, we will realize that negative feelings arose within the perpetrator first. He was disturbed by the other person first. He suffered first. Though he deserves to be blessed, he receives curses. Hence, it is essential to accept the angry one first, forgive him for his anger, and send him healing rays with blessings, certainly not curses.

Forgiving is an important aspect of healing rays. When the angry one receives the medicine of forgiveness, the healing process starts within him, and gradually his anger begins to mellow down.

When one comes to know that certain food contains bad bacteria, he avoids eating it and prevents his family from eating it. Similarly, when one gets convinced that curses only harm, he will send healing rays instead of curses to all, which will then positively touch everyone.

When everyone in the world can understand this unseen secret, then all the needy people will start receiving healing and blessings. As a result, they will attain mental wellbeing. Besides this, their karmic disease will get annihilated instead of intensifying. This will not only harmonize relationships for the better, but also open the possibility of a new life filled with love and bliss for all.

12

Nature – the Greatest Healer

You could have surely heard of the proverb, "Time is the best healer." Time heals all wounds, be it physical or mental. But have you ever reflected on what exactly happens with the passing of time? Does the situation change, or does our sorrow reduce with the passage of time? Who heals our wounds?

It is nature. Yes, nature is the greatest healer! It is nature's wonder how our painful memories fade away over time.

At the mental level, you would have experienced how you are relieved of almost all your memories gradually, whether they are happy or hurtful ones. All memories are cast away with time.

Pleasant memories leave a wave of joy that one does not want to let go of, whereas painful memories leave a sting behind that one does not want to remember. It is essential to be free from both these kinds of memories to experience lasting happiness and contentment. Nature beautifully arranges for this whereby we don't need to do anything, and we forget everything automatically.

Nature wants to heal everyone. Hence, everyone is naturally attracted to good health. Some illnesses get cured with time. We are constantly guided to progress towards good health and bring about changes in our diet. Nature encourages us to include those food items in our diet that help us attain good health.

The more we stay attuned with nature, the easier it becomes for us to attain good health. On the contrary, the more we get into discord with nature, the more our health deteriorates. Every animal gets to eat what makes it healthy. If any animal falls sick, nature has its arrangement to heal it too. In short, nature has made everything available for everyone to keep fit, provided they reach out to it.

Nature functions by its laws. Its healing power is constantly eradicating diseases. It is continually renewing and replenishing the old with the new—be it human beings, birds and animals, or trees and plants. All this is ceaselessly happening in an auto-mode without any external intervention.

Humans are the only creatures on Earth who create their world through their thoughts and get entrapped in the cycle of joy and sorrow. However, nature has provided such an arrangement that even the human body has the power to heal itself. All body tissue, including bones, hair, and skin, automatically replenish themselves without our conscious awareness. However, humans suffer due to the karmic diseases caused by their negative thoughts. Nature intends to heal those karmic wounds as well, provided one patiently allows nature to do its part and becomes instrumental for spreading its healing power to others.

For this, we need to be open to feel nature's power being showered upon us and received within us. We need to imagine that we are becoming pure and healthy with nature's divine light. Then, we need to radiate the same healing light and healing words to others with the understanding that nature is making us a medium to heal others physically and mentally.

When we become instrumental for sending healing rays to others, we experience joy and peace. Let us understand how we can send healing rays to others.

1. Sit down at a quiet place in a comfortable posture for some time.

2. Imagine that white light is being showered upon you from the Universe, and you are being filled with it.

3. Now, imagine the person, whom you wish to send healing rays, sitting right in front of you.

4. Verbalize and visualize these healing words, "Divine white light is being showered on you, and you are completely healed. All the negativity within you has dissolved in this divine light. You are freed from karmic disease. You have become completely healthy and are filled with love, joy, and peace."

5. Peacefully rest in this state for some time and feel that you are the medium to transmit the divine healing light being showered upon you from the Universe to the person sitting in front of you.

6. Continue to sit in this state for some time, with a feeling of gratitude. In the end, thank nature's healing power in the form of the divine light and the other person.

Sending healing rays in this manner will not only benefit the other person but yourself too. You will benefit from the divine light; your level of consciousness will rise.

When the sunrays envelop the earth, the world gets filled with its light; trees blossom, the darkness of the night disappears. In much the same way, when we send healing rays with blessings to someone, their lives also begin to brighten. Their karmic disease begins to get eradicated.

Nevertheless, what does the sun *do* to spread light on the earth? The sun only showers its light, without any bias. It doesn't differentiate, "This person is bad. Hence I will not shower my light upon him." All receive the same light in the same measure from the sun.

Humans are akin to the sun. They are the source of divine light. Hence, when we send healing rays, we get self-illumined; we become the medium for healing. Thus, we help giving healing rays to everyone. When we bestow benevolent, compassionate rays upon everyone, those rays illumine their lives, they receive healing, and their problems begin to dissolve!

13

Qualities Required to Send Healing Rays

Having understood the importance of healing rays, you must be eager to cast its light on yourself and others. But before sending healing rays, it is essential to understand the qualities, the mental state, the inner strength, and the kind of feelings required to forgive others for their mistakes and pray for them.

Most people generally follow the principle of "Tit for Tat." "If the other person misbehaves with me, I will also pay him back in the same coin," this is their mindset. In such a situation, far from sending healing rays, they cannot forgive each other.

Hence, if we want to benefit from the power of healing rays in our life and become instrumental for others, we need to nurture the required qualities. These qualities inspire us to positively contribute to heal every situation and problem by sending healing rays.

These qualities are like the three blades of a ceiling fan that spin around the fixed rod in the center, enabling the fan to blow air.

These three qualities are awareness, responsibility, and courage. The central fixed rod is a steadfast and peaceful mind. Let us understand these qualities in detail.

1. Awareness

One, who is constantly aware of everything happening around him, who can retain his level of awareness during and after challenging incidents, starts sending healing rays immediately. Neither does he need to be reminded nor does he delay sitting in meditation for doing that.

If he sees an ambulance passing by, he immediately sends healing rays for the sick person and his family members. If he is amidst an ongoing family dispute, as soon as he gathers his awareness, he mentally seeks forgiveness from all the concerned people in the family and sends healing rays to them so that the dispute ends soon. Thus, retaining a high level of awareness is a prerequisite for sending healing rays to people in times of their need.

2. Responsibility

Though we are not to be blamed for whatever happens around us, yet we are responsible for it. There is a difference between "being blamed" and "being responsible." If not by speech or actions, we may have contributed to the incident through our feelings and thoughts at a subtle level. The happening of the incident in front of us testifies that we are party to it. We become responsible as witnessers to the incident. This makes us even more responsible for sending healing rays so that all the people, including us, get healed. Realizing the sense of responsibility makes it easy to send healing rays.

Imagine that you are watching a movie in a theatre. Suddenly a child begins to cry in the auditorium. Some people get irritated and shout, "For God's sake, can someone silence that child? We're unable to hear anything. That kid is spoiling the fun." Some others become angry at these irritating people and say, "Let the child cry, but why are you making noise on top of it?" Thus, the entire atmosphere becomes chaotic and disturbed. Everyone creates karmic bondage with the other. It's as if the karmic disease spreads like fire.

Some people quietly observe whatever is going on. They remain neutral as they don't contribute in any way. But if you too are part of the audience in that theatre, what would you do?

First, you would own the responsibility for whatever is happening around you. Then, you would begin sending healing rays to the child and the audience, "Calm down! Everything will be fine. A small child does cry. It's not a big deal." This is a positive contribution. This would make the child's parents think of taking the child out and help the atmosphere calm down. Thus, mentally verbalizing such words with love and sending healing rays from your side could resolve the problem, provided you take responsibility for it.

3. Courage

The courage that we are discussing here is spiritual courage, not physical courage. We need spiritual courage to persevere and retain a high level of consciousness consistently. Operating from this high level of consciousness will then render us the courage to forgive others and send them healing rays. Attaining spiritual wisdom helps us gain spiritual courage.

With spiritual wisdom, we realize that God alone exists in all living and non-living beings. God is enacting various roles through each body in this worldly drama. Whatever actions are performed by each body are based on their level of consciousness and understanding. Action being the same, it may be regarded wrong by one with a higher level of consciousness and right by the other with a lower level of consciousness. This means whether an action is right or wrong depends on the level of consciousness of the one perceiving it. In this way, whatever happens to anyone depends on their level of consciousness; no one can be blamed for it. Everyone is merely performing their role based on the thoughts arising within them.

With this understanding, it becomes easy to forgive people for their so-called mistakes. As our level of consciousness rises, we begin to perceive others from this perspective, forgive them, and send them healing rays. Hence, we should start raising our level of consciousness to become spiritually courageous.

Besides these qualities, one needs to have qualities like love, joy, and compassion to make them worthy of sending healing rays. Each one of us has these qualities in abundance within us from birth. When these qualities were received at the time of birth, we were pure. But with time, we got tainted with the grime of negative tendencies. We need to cleanse ourselves of this grime and become courageous.

With the rise in our level of consciousness, these qualities automatically begin to blossom. And the more these qualities unfold, the more our level of awareness rises on its own. We find ourselves in harmony with who we truly are – the true Self.

When we function from this supreme pure state and send healing rays, it positively influences other person's thoughts, just as it happened with the people resting under the shade of the extraordinary tree. Owing to the blessings backed with pure feelings received from the tree, travelers would feel good; they would get solutions to their problems and connect with the true Self.

Hence, we need to realize our true nature and start working towards abiding in the higher level of consciousness. This will enable us to unleash the hidden qualities of love, joy, and compassion within us and make ourselves capable of sending healing rays for the welfare of people.

14

The Three P's – Prescribe, Pray, and Proclaim

It is essential to understand what feelings we should harbor for sending healing rays effectively. As these feelings and their effects happen in the unseen, we fail to understand them.

Consider, you visit a cinema to watch a three-dimensional (3D) movie, and the movie has already begun. As you have not yet worn the special 3D glasses, you cannot comprehend the three dimensions of the movie. As soon as you put on the glasses, you get to watch the 3D effects of the movie.

In much the same way, you need to put on a special set of 3D glasses—the glasses of understanding—in your life to be able to comprehend the essential feelings required for sending healing rays. The three dimensions that unfold with the glasses of understanding are the three P's. Let us understand them in detail.

1. Prescribe the medicine of patience, attention, and gratitude

In our daily life, we deal with many people and use many things; our life would have been very difficult without them. We know about their importance in our life. Yet we often forget this aspect and tend to use things carelessly or behave rudely with people. We never think of thanking them.

We should have feelings of gratitude for them, which work like medicine. Our relationships begin to heal when we thank people, pay attention to them, and behave patiently with them. The medicine comprising patience, attention, and gratitude helps relieve tensions and resolve conflicts in relationships. Similarly, when we pay attention to our belongings every now and then, lovingly caress them, and thank them, they serve us in the best manner. In this way, paying attention, listening, behaving with patience, and being grateful is like sending healing rays.

Very often, we don't give due importance to these aspects. We don't feel the need to express gratitude for these aspects. Let us understand this with the example of the 3D movie itself. While watching the movie, do we feel grateful for being able to watch it? No, we don't! We may initially feel a sense of wonder and gratitude, but watching the movie becomes a casual affair for us in due course. Without making any special efforts, we simply decide to watch it.

We never think of the efforts that have gone into making the movie. Hence, we don't feel grateful for watching the marvelous movie. We simply consider it as a transaction. But someone has taken efforts to make this movie. So many people have contributed their best towards its creation! When we remember all this, we begin to appreciate it. Had we been told to make the movie ourselves and then watch it, how would it be? Reflect whether it would have been ever possible for us. Such reflection will awaken the feeling of gratitude for those who have creatively made the movie.

In the same manner, some people have dedicated their lives to discover certain medicines. We merely purchase them but generally don't feel gratitude towards them. This is so because we think, "I have paid money and purchased the medicines." However, we are unaware of the efforts spent since decades to discover and formulate the medicines. Hence, we don't feel grateful for having them. But hereon, we can be aware of such subtle aspects and appreciate the smallest of things with a feeling of gratitude. When we feel gratitude and thank people, we spread healing rays. Therefore, develop the quality of sending healing rays to others through the medicine of patience, attention, and gratitude.

2. Pray

How do you feel when you pray for someone? What feelings do you experience? For sure, you would feel happy and contented. These feelings are healing rays that reach out to the other person. If someone is angry at you or some other person, and you pray, "May he be at peace," then these healing rays reach out to him.

You wouldn't have been able to pray this way without knowing about healing rays. But with this knowledge, you realize that the angry person needs your prayers and not your resentment.

Thus, only after you gain knowledge and awareness can you send healing rays in the form of prayers to others. Every religion has given a lot of importance to prayers. When we pray to God with a pure mind for someone, it touches the other person positively, and our mind also becomes pure.

3. Proclaim

If someone overtakes you on the road and goes ahead, how do you react? Do you retort in anger, "Why is he in such a hurry? Doesn't he value his life? He will end up killing himself as well as others."? Or do you pray for him, "Relax. Go slow. All your tasks will be completed at the right time."?

Whatever statements you make during daily situations are your proclamations. Now, you need to become proficient at converting them into prayer-like proclamations.

Proclamations are statements made in full faith, and proficiency is skilled expertise. Proficiency in proclamations implies gaining expertise in sending healing prayers to people. Whatever healing statements you say for people, say them with full faith. Some wise masters are so proficient that all that they assert prove to be true. All the saints were so proficient in sending healing rays that their blessings would bear fruit. Therefore, people would seek their blessings before starting any auspicious work.

Similarly, the practice of sending healing rays should get so deeply imbibed within you that you can see their effects yourself; your healing statements will come true. To reach this state, you need to practice sending healing rays consistently, with awareness, to others in everyday situations. Let this practice deepen so that it becomes your nature. You then become proficient in sending healing rays.

When you consciously use the 3D glasses of the three P's, namely: prescription, prayers, and proclamation, you will witness the magic of healing rays in your life as well as that of others. Thus, by sending healing rays, not only will you improve your relationships and harmonize with your things, but wherever you go, you will contribute significantly to healing the incidents and problems of people around you.

15

Shoot the Arrows of Healing Rays

A pure, simple, and open mind is essential for sending healing rays to people. You would have heard the saying, "The mind is like a parachute. It's of no use unless it is open." An open mind is required even for sending healing rays to people.

You can imagine the consequences if someone were to jump from a flying aircraft with a parachute and the parachute doesn't open at all. Similarly, we have received our physical body along with the mind, and we can progress and help others progress only when we open our mind.

The open mind implies a flexible mind which doesn't immediately discard anything it hears for the first time. For example, if someone says, "One can lead a natural and simple life with love, joy, and peace," then instead of rejecting it outright, an open mind seeks to understand.

Those who have an open mind, who easily assimilate the new, have a flexible intellect. They can be called "Benevolent Seekers" because they are open to seek within, and they trust goodness and truthfulness.

Many people have a closed mind because they consider whatever they believe to be the undoubtable truth. If someone tells them something new, they are unable to accept it. They say, "No, this cannot be! How can transformation happen by just sending healing rays? Why should I send healing rays to someone I dislike? Is there really something like this so-called extraordinary law? If someone has ill-treated me, I should pay him back in the same coin. I should teach him a lesson," and so on. Such people can even go as far as becoming fanatics or terrorists. Such a diseased mind can be called a "Malevolent sufferer."

Such sufferers need treatment. Benevolent seekers need to work for their healing. They need to send them healing rays so that the medicine can reach out to them in the form of blessings.

A closed mind would say, "What will happen with just one thought, one prayer, or by just sending healing rays?" If one is told, "Even if no one in the world is sending healing rays, you can still start sending them," his closed mind would say, "What's the use? What will happen with a single person's thoughts?" He is unable to have faith and gather courage because of his closed mind.

When one is treated badly or unfairly, generally, one thinks of retaliating. Most people tend to harbor revengeful feelings. They fail to envisage that there could be another way, another aspect that could be for the wellbeing of all, serving everyone's interests.

But those with an open mind will contemplate, "If this is being said, there could be some truth in it which I am unable to grasp right now. Perhaps it might carry a hidden secret that few are aware of, and hence very few are able to have faith in it." Besides their open mind, such people also possess one more quality – the courage to accept the truth, which at times seems to defy logic. Due to this, they are able to have faith in the unseen laws of healing rays and the unseen effects of blessings. As a result, they begin sending healing rays.

Thus, besides an open mind, the quality of courage is also required. People are unable to gather courage. They are afraid of contemplating their own beliefs and confronting the truth. Those who can gather courage are able to forego their wrong beliefs, adopt new ways, and begin to send healing rays for the wellbeing of all.

Let's understand this in depth with the help of a story.

In the story, two benevolent people face off with each other on the battlefield due to differences in their perspectives on some topic. As we know, when two people differ in their perspectives, they jovially say, "Let's wage a battle. The perspective of whoever wins will prevail." Thus, both decide to battle.

Now, both are benevolent at the outset. No one is wrong. Otherwise, whenever we think of a battle, we assume that one is right and the other wrong. But here, both are right; both are benevolent, just their perspectives differ.

The battle begins. The first person shoots an arrow which causes an invisible scar of karmic bondage. The second person also shoots an arrow, and that too creates a scar of karmic bondage. Thus, arrows are shot from both sides. From both sides, karmic bondage is created. The battle continues from morning till night. Indian television viewers may have seen such scenes in the mythological serials like Ramayana and Mahabharata, wherein one arrow is shot from one side and the other from the other side. They both collide in the sky. This scene continues throughout the day.

As the arrow is shot from the bow, the one who shoots also experiences a jolt as the bow recoils. Thus, the arrow affects not only the one it is shot at but also the one who shoots.

The two warriors settle down for the evening. Both the people were benevolent in the morning. During the entire day, they were waging war. When they retire for the night, none of them is benevolent, there are only revengeful sufferers on both sides! Both have become like the demonic Ravana. Both have forgotten who they truly are and have believed the war to be their defining truth. This was the first scene.

In the second scene, the benevolent companions gather at the battlefield, and the battle begins. The first one shoots an arrow creating a scar of karmic bondage. The second one also retaliates, causing further bondage. But something changes in the afternoon. One of them remembers a deeper truth of who they are and why they are present in the battlefield. When he shoots an arrow, instead of creating a scar of bondage, a healing ray is sent across. A scar of bondage is sent from one side, but it is met by a healing ray from the other side! Scar of bondage, healing ray... Scar of bondage, healing ray... This way, the battle goes on during the entire day. In the evening, onlookers find Ravana on one side and Lord Rama on the other! Here the second scene comes to an end.

Now in the third scene, the benevolent duo face off on the battlefield. One has shot an arrow causing a scar of bondage, and the other has sent a healing ray. In this scene, healing rays are sent from one side from the very beginning of the day, and scars of bondage are inflicted from the other side. It's like a healing ray, a scar of bondage... A healing ray, a scar of bondage...

In the second scene, healing rays were sent in the afternoon. But in the third scene, they are sent from the morning itself. What is the outcome? In the afternoon, the one who was shooting arrows of karmic bondage also begins sending healing rays! Now, the healing rays are being sent from both sides. What will happen in the evening? At sunset, both the warriors come together and embrace each other, "I am Lord Rama, and so are you... You are Rama, and I am Rama too." Both become one, and the demonism of Ravana is eliminated.

Now, the dynamics of the battle has entirely changed. The war is a divine game of joy between Rama One and Rama Two! Healing rays are sent across at each other. What kind of a battle is this? "I am Rama... I am Rama too... I love you... I love you too... I am an incarnation of the divine... and so are you!"

This story has deep symbolism. In the story, both are benevolent; both are Lord Rama—divine oneness. But in due course, they begin to wrongly believe themselves as Ravana—separate individuals limited to their body-mind. They fight with each other to prove themselves right and superior to the other.

The shooting of arrows symbolizes cursing others due to karmic disease, using the arrows of wrong words, "I am like this... You are like that... I am a tiger... You are a swine... I am right... You are wrong..." These arrows inflict invisible scars of bondage, which aggravates their karmic disease.

We also need to reflect on what we have considered ourselves as while interacting with others. Do we believe ourselves to be separate individuals, limited to our bodies? And what is the outcome of this belief.

Regardless of whoever initiated the debate or battle, in the end, only Ravana – the symbol of hatred – dwells within both. Both develop vengeance, which gets further fueled in battle. Hence, both continue to behave hatefully with each other. In short, their karmic bondage increases, and so do the resultant karmic scars.

In the second scene, in the afternoon, one of them awakens to a remembrance that his original nature is that of benevolence, and so is the other's nature. Then he begins to send healing rays. This is because he has realized that he should speak and act according to what he wishes to create in his own life. He needs to awaken the other person. Although the other person keeps sending arrows of bondage, he begins to send healing rays because of his renewed understanding.

In the third scene, as one of them has awakened since morning, he feels compassion for the other person. Only blessings and benevolent feelings arise within him for the other person with the pure intention that he too should awaken and realize his divine nature; that he too is Lord Rama, not Ravana.

After attaining this understanding, you, too, start sending healing rays of love and blessings to all. Even if the other person misbehaves with you, you still need to keep sending healing rays only to awaken divinity within him. The rays will have their healing effect on him. The effect is unseen and hence not visible initially. It is most likely that the other person's behavior won't change immediately. And yet, you still need to keep sending healing rays. Your persistence in sending healing rays will bring about a transformation within him in due course of time. Gradually, he will awaken, just as it happened with the other person in the third scene.

Now, keep the book aside for some time and contemplate the situations from your daily life where you would use this understanding. Consider which people you will send healing rays to. As you start practicing this, you will find that all the hatred gives way to a feeling of love and compassion. You become the source of peace. Being in this state, you would want to send healing rays to all beings and usher peace in the world. There is so much power in healing rays that it can help avert war between nations.

Contemplate deeply on this story and make the best use of healing rays in your life. Strengthen yourself first by becoming benevolent so that you can awaken the benevolence and divine remembrance within others.

While sending healing rays to others, tell yourself, "I am benevolent, and so are you! I am an expression of the divine, and so are you!" In this way, you will be able to experience the magic of healing rays not only in your life but in the lives of others too.

16
Benefits of Healing Rays

When we send healing rays, our mind becomes pure and sacred. Such a mind makes it easy for us to respond with divine devotion even in the most challenging situations. We start becoming free from our ingrained tendencies. This increases our focus during meditation. Hence, we should draw the utmost benefit of opportunities for sending healing rays.

Let us understand the benefits of sending healing rays in detail.

1. Renders mental and physical health

In the ordinary course, sending healing rays appears to be merely a positive action. However, the very intent of sending healing rays acts as a powerful shield, safeguarding us from karmic disease. Generally, our mind gets tainted with negative feelings like hatred, jealousy, malice, anger, fear, resentment, and worry. The energy sent in the form of healing rays renders mental and physical health not only to the recipient but also the sender. Healing happens at such a deep level of our inner being that our conscience gains purity and clarity.

2. Eases meditation

Sending healing rays settles the volatile, reactive, and restless state of mind. A pure and sacred mind gets easily absorbed in the peaceful state of meditation.

The practice of meditation, in turn, makes us compassionate and loving towards those who triggered our anger, sorrow, or distress earlier. An aura of benevolence gets created around us. Every cell in the body is filled with love. This can be called "love loaded pulse." We verbalize only words of blessings for others. The intensity of our karmic disease reduces, and healing rays automatically emanate through us.

We earn the merit of inner strength and the radiance of pure consciousness. The practice of meditation strengthens our spiritual foundation, due to which wrong deeds stop happening through us. It puts an end to actions, speech, feelings, and thoughts that emerge from ignorance. We start leading a divine life.

3. Helps to give the right response

Our old tendencies provoke us to react egoistically, resulting in karmic bondage. The habit of sending healing rays helps break these tendencies and enables us to respond afresh. As a result, karmic bondage begins to dissolve. Our nature gets transformed. Thus, sending healing rays not only makes small changes in our life but improves the very fabric of our life.

4. Enhances spiritual power

We need to attain strength in all the four facets of life—spiritual, mental, intellectual, and physical.

We all wish to possess all kinds of powers. We want our feelings, thoughts, speech, and actions to be extremely potent to help us attain whatever we desire. But we cannot achieve this by mere wishing. We need to increase our spiritual strength. The practice of consistently sending healing rays serves as a catalyst for this.

Besides, this practice purifies our aura, making it radiant like that of a child. The aura of a child is pure, powerful, and resplendent. We can sense it from a distance before we come close to the child. But as the child grows up, spiritual lethargy and deviousness begin to gradually set in, dulling and diminishing the aura. If one pays attention to developing spiritual strength, the aura will never fade.

17
Improving Relationships with Healing Rays

Man is a social being. As soon as he is born, he gets bound in several relationships that keep him enmeshed throughout his life. His experiences in these relationships condition him and shape his personality, thus becoming the cause of his happiness as well as sorrow.

Although relationships are meant for sharing our joy, they often become the cause of our suffering. Very often, relationships become so sour and strained that they inflict karmic disease.

Consider a fourteen-year-old boy who shares his daily experiences with his mother after returning from school. One day he tells her, "Tomorrow, I have been summoned to the principal's office." When his mother enquires, he explains, "My friends challenged me to tease a girl by whistling at her. As soon as she entered the class, I did it, only to stand up to their challenge. During the recess, I also tried smoking a cigarette at their insistence and was caught by a teacher who was passing by."

The boy honestly and innocently shares everything with his mother, but his mother gets angry and scolds him. She then shares this with her husband. The husband admonishes the boy by shouting at him, "Were you born only to show us this day? This way, you are doomed!" and so on.

Hearing such harsh and bitter words from his parents, the simple, straightforward, innocent boy gets scared. He thinks, "I have committed such a grave and unpardonable crime. I am the cause of my parent's sorrow. Indeed, I am good-for-nothing." This guilt consumes the boy within. Gradually, he begins to mentally distance himself from his parents. In ignorance, the parents create a negative barrier within the boy's mind.

Such children can continue their wrongdoings outside but stop confiding in their parents about it. The parents live in the illusion that their children have mended their ways after their scolding. But their children feel estranged from their parents and often fall into the wrong company.

Had the parents been aware, they would have never said, "You are wrong." Instead, they would have befriended their children and lovingly discussed the matter with them. They would have said, "We have also experimented during our school days, but later we realized our mistakes," or "We have closely observed the consequences of such things in our life. Therefore, it will help to refrain from such habits as soon as possible for a brighter future. We are always with you, no matter what. Don't worry; together, we will help you break this habit."

In other words, they make the child feel, "*You* are not wrong, but your *action* is wrong. You are good, but the habit of eve-teasing or smoking cigarettes is bad."

When children are told that they are not wrong, but rather their habits and actions, then there is a possibility that they detach themselves from such vices and avoid them in the future.

Parents should accept their children as they are and send healing rays to them. They should become friendly guides to their children and impress upon them what is appropriate and undesirable. The children can then become their parents' fans! They will maintain proximity with their parents and keep away from wrong deeds. With their parent's guidance, they can also understand other relations better and move ahead in life by maintaining harmony in their relationships.

This change in the approach of parents towards their children is not just limited to the parent-child relationship. One can reflect on their other relationships in the same manner. One always finds faults with others due to a lack of right understanding. They create karmic bondage in their relationships through their behavior and fall prey to karmic disease.

There are all kinds of people in a family. Everyone has their set thinking pattern, habits, and behavior. Instead of sending healing rays to strengthen these relations, man distances himself from others with his harsh and sarcastic behavior. He believes the other person is the cause of the rift and speaks ill of that person. This spreads the karmic disease in turn, and he experiences conflict, discord, and unhappiness in relationships. Such spoilt relationships can improve by sending healing rays.

Trivial disputes do happen in a husband-wife relationship. In such cases, they should immediately discuss together, seek forgiveness, and forgive each other to resolve the conflict. But the converse happens. The wife continues to grumble, "He is more bothered about his own family members. He doesn't care about me or my family. He always does what he wants without considering me," and so on.

In this case, the wife can send healing rays, "He takes care of everyone and helps me too. All problems are getting resolved peacefully. Love, joy, peace, and satisfaction is blossoming in our relationship," and so on.

Mentally verbalizing healing words can stop karmic disease before it aggravates. It can strengthen the bonding in relationships.

We can apply the same understanding in sibling relationships too. Just as, after a quarrel, the sister complains about her brother, "Nowadays he just keeps to himself. He doesn't pay heed to me.

He's not bothered about even calling me up. He just caters to his wife's fancies," and so on.

If there are disputes between siblings over property matters, they can make use of healing words such as, "We are born under one roof to lovingly live together. We live in harmony and care for one another. We all have an abundance of health, wealth, and time. We all get along very well with everyone. Together we are living a fulfilled life."

If healing rays are sent in the same manner in other disturbed relationships, those relationships will improve and flourish with love, joy, and peace. Karmic disease will get eradicated completely.

The relationship between a mother-in-law and daughter-in-law, or between two sisters-in-law, is exceptionally delicate, especially in a typically prevalent Indian family setup. These relationships and their surrounding belief systems trigger quarrels in the family. Instead of observing the shortcomings in each other, if healing rays are sent, "There is peace, love, and joy at home. Everyone is in harmony with the other," then the home can become a heaven.

One verbalizes negative words for his relations knowingly or unknowingly, due to which karmic disease spreads. Sending healing rays to them can put an end to all this.

When one learns to live in harmony with their family members based on the right understanding, they will be able to repeat them same in the outside world too. Whenever they witness something undesirable taking place, they will immediately send healing rays. In this way, they will become instrumental in creating a highly evolved society.

18

Changing Behavior with Healing Rays

Suppose you are starving since morning. You have just found time to open your lunch box and are about to eat. Suddenly your friend comes in and grabs a sandwich from your lunch box and leaves. How would you respond? Would your hunger be replaced by anger!? Would you abuse and curse him? Or would you bless and wish him well?

Usually, one could get upset and mentally curse him with words like, "You grabbed my sandwich when I was hungry… May you suffer indigestion… You should fall sick," and so forth.

Each person's nature is different. Some people would laugh it off as a trivial incident. Some may choose to disregard it and let go. They will react aggressively to something only if it causes them significant loss. Some people tide through even the biggest losses cheerfully and send healing rays in return. Thus, each person's nature reflects in their thoughts and their subsequent reactions to situations.

Human nature doesn't get formed overnight. One inherits behavioral traits from parents. Whatever one observes and hears from parents, teachers, neighbors, friends, and society from childhood conditions his mind. For example, when he hears his father say, "People are mean and selfish. They cater to wealthy people only," he too develops an attitude towards people. When he watches people blaming God for their fate, he gets influenced by it.

His nature gets molded by the good and bad things he has observed in his surroundings since his childhood. He, too, loses faith in people. His distrust stops him from taking any initiative to help others. When someone needs help, he either escapes from that situation or makes excuses.

His negative thinking makes him criticize others, count their weaknesses and the losses incurred in every situation. As a result, he fails to adapt to anything new. Safeguarding himself by giving excuses and criticizing others becomes his inherent nature. This causes karmic bondage and aggravates his karmic disease. As most people are ignorant about this, they don't feel the need or urgency to change their nature. Even if they want to, they consider it impossible.

But it is indeed possible to change our nature! We can change our nature with some effort and resolve. We can bring about a change in our condition by sending healing rays to *ourselves* and others. Even by rendering little help to others, we can begin to eradicate our karmic disease.

If we firmly resolve to change our nature, then it is very much possible. For this, we need to take some small steps first that are immediately possible.

Feelings and thoughts are invisible. Hence, it is safer to first work on them. When we work on our our feelings and thoughts, it also transforms our speech and actions. Even if we commit any mistake by feeling negatively or thinking wrongly about someone out of habit, we can mentally seek forgiveness from them. We will, no doubt, commit such mistakes due to our old nature, but we can immediately correct them by practicing forgiveness. As we become increasingly aware of our feelings and thoughts over time, these mistakes will gradually reduce and come to an end. We will harbor only benevolent feelings and happy thoughts for others.

When we have pure feelings for people, then our thoughts also become pure. We speak sweet, loving words, which gradually cascade into our actions as well.

You may have heard or read stories of great masters. The sublime state that they dwelled in, their deep benevolence for all beings not only reflected in their feelings and thoughts but also cascaded to their speech and actions. When we read their biographies, we wonder, "How could they speak and act like that?"

Once, the Indian medieval Saint Namdev was very hungry. He opened his lunch packet to have his meal. Suddenly, a dog came running, picked up a *roti* (bread) from his packet in its jaws, and ran away. Now, Saint Namdev began running after the dog, not to pelt stones at it, but to plead, "O my Lord! Why are you eating the dry roti? Let me apply some butter on it. Please don't go without it." People were observing him. His purity of mind and affection for all beings were evident in his speech and action.

Many people consider that he could speak and act this way only because he was a saint. But we need to understand why he could do it, what was the understanding that made it possible for him. What kind of satisfaction did he experience by *not* having the roti and feeding the dog instead?

The feeling with which he could speak and act with such compassion is our true nature. Our true nature is love, joy, and eternal silence. But we have forgotten it and are leading our lives based on a false identity that we have assumed for ourselves. The very purpose of our life on Earth is to return to our true nature.

If you are able to bless the person who has taken away your food by saying words like, "What you have taken away is delicious. My mother has lovingly prepared it. You will feel healthy and contented after having it," then these words are healing rays.

It is a law of nature—Whatever we give, returns to us multiplied many times. Whether we send healing rays or curses, both return to us multifold. Hence, we are not doing a favor on anyone by sending healing rays; rather, we are working for our own well-being. This will not only help the other person but primarily transform our own nature.

When someone steals your bread, you can also send healing rays to them by saying, "The bread you are consuming is rightfully yours. You can earn your bread. You don't need to depend on others for that. May you receive an abundance of love, joy, wealth, time, food, and comforts."

Saint Namdev could harbor such feelings even for a dog, and it reflected in his speech and actions. Let this begin with our feelings and thoughts. If someone does something wrong for the sake of bread, it means that he doesn't feel capable of earning a living. He lacks the faith, "I can earn it." You send him healing rays by saying, "You don't need to do something wrong for the sake of bread. May you always get enough food to satisfy your need. You are capable. You are an angel. You are an aspect of God. May God bless you with wisdom and me too."

When you send healing rays in this manner, you become the source of healing and are filled with powerful vibrations of benevolence and gratitude. This makes it conducive for you to return to your true nature and abide in it.

When a situation is challenging, we should at least be conscious enough to entertain benevolent feelings. Wherever possible, we can verbalize them. We may perhaps find this difficult to start with. We may get irritated and feel like abusing the other person. Despite this, we need to try and verbalize positive statements to send healing rays. Words have the power to alter our feelings. When we verbalize positive words of benevolence, our feelings will also gradually get attuned with them.

We need inner strength to respond anew. For that, we need to practice meditation daily. We need to keep sending healing rays through our feelings, thoughts, and consciously chosen words to ourselves as well as others. When we get established in our true nature of love, joy, and peace, then our presence, by itself, will serve as healing rays for others!

19
Sympathy and Compassion

Sympathy and compassion are not mere words but invisible feelings that can significantly transform one's life. There is a subtle difference between sympathy and compassion.

When we feel sympathetic for someone, we may exclaim, "Poor fellow! He is a victim of his situation!" However, we don't realize a negative undertone in such pitying that further lowers his already lowered state.

At a subtle level, pity or sympathy is like judging ourselves or others as weak or fragile. Those who are sympathized, sense it at the subconscious level. If they are not aware, they may even get influenced by such pity and start believing that they are victims of circumstances rather than creators of their life.

When we feel compassionate for someone, we pray for their wellbeing and exclaim, "God bless them." Compassion fills the mind with love and hope, whereas sympathy causes a feeling of helplessness. Thus, sympathy carries a negative undertone to some extent, whereas compassion brings about purity and positivity in the mind.

For example, if a king has forgotten his true identity and believes himself to be a beggar, you too regard him as a beggar and sympathize with him. But when you know that he is a king and has forgotten his true identity, you will feel compassion for him. Sympathy arises from ignorance of our true nature, whereas compassion arises from awareness of the grandeur of our true nature.

Let us now understand how we can transmute our sympathy into compassion.

When we see someone who is sick, we feel sympathy for them. We spontaneously comment, "He's unable to sit or stand. What a pathetic state the poor fellow is in!" On witnessing an accident, we may think, "That was terrible! Don't know whether anyone has survived at all."

Such thoughts arise from human sensitivity. They convey feelings that are intrinsic to human nature. Such feelings indicate that we wish for the other person's wellbeing, that his condition improves, and he be relieved of grief and pain. This is the popular meaning of sympathy that we all know.

But do such feelings really help them? No! These are feelings of pity, not compassion. Many people believe that if we say a few sympathetic words to someone or inquire about a sick person's wellbeing, then we have done our duty; we can't do anything beyond that.

But sympathy is truly backed by compassion only when our actions also align with our words. This happens when we help someone with some money, in-kind, or at their work, or when we express healing words through our thoughts and feelings and pray for them. When we wish for their good health, abundance, and happiness with a pure mind, these feelings reach out to them. They bring happiness and prosperity to their lives.

With compassion, we consider the other person as an aspect of God and send him healing rays. We pray for his growth using words like, "Let him receive the very best in abundance according to his divine plan." When we empathize with an understanding of his divine nature and the potential of power that lies latent within him, it takes the pure form of compassion.

Let each person receive whatever is right and best according to his divine plan. This means that he should be forgiven for the wrong deeds he performed through his feelings, thoughts, speech, and actions, as well as the karmic disease created by him. Also, he should reap the fruits of his good karma and progress on the path to freedom from karmic bondage.

All parents wish that their children experience all the happiness in their lives. They strive hard to fulfill all their desires and keep blessing them. They accumulate wealth for their children so that the children do not have to face any problems. They leave behind all their wealth for their children through their will so that the children can live comfortably and happily. Just as parents do not think ill for their children, God—the father of the universe—also wishes to give everything in abundance to everyone.

The divine plan is that everything is available in abundance for each one of us. There is abundant sunlight, water, air, plants, trees, and forests in nature. Our bodies are the expression of divine intelligence – a wondrous mechanism at work. The human body has billions of cells that specialize in various physiological functions. In short, God has created everything in abundance for everyone in nature.

If everything is in abundance, then why doesn't it reach out to all? It's due to karmic bondage and karmic disease caused by negative feelings and thoughts.

Knowingly or unknowingly, we create hurdles in the fruition of our divine plan by entertaining negative feelings and thoughts. As a result, the best possibilities that were moving towards manifestation in our lives stop midway. Our mind and self-talk are the biggest "factories" that produce karmic bondage. They keep creating karmic bondage, which then aggravates karmic disease within us.

Let us understand this with some examples:

- In a family, people create karmic bondage by quarreling among themselves and mentally cursing one another.
- As we walk along the street or watch TV, we mentally condemn the government.
- We regard someone stupid if he lacks road traffic discipline.
- We consider shopkeepers as cunning and deceitful.
- Many people speak negatively about their housemaids or subordinate colleagues.

Unknown to us, all of this keeps aggravating karmic disease within and around us.

When our karmic disease intensifies, divine grace cannot reach us. Therefore, we need to first cleanse ourselves within by using healing words and practicing forgiveness. We need to pray, "According to my divine plan, let all karmic bondage be eradicated from my life. Please free me from karmic disease. Let my life take a positive turn." Our karmic disease begins to fade away by praying with persistence, and the best possibilities that are meant to manifest by the divine plan begin to flow freely in our life.

Just as we pray for ourselves, we should also pray for others, "Let everyone receive whatever they wish or better according to their divine plan. May their karmic bondage be eradicated. Let them be freed from karmic disease according to their divine plan."

When we pray for ourselves and others in this manner, we too become worthy of compassion. Besides becoming free from karmic bondage, we also become instrumental in opening the doors for liberation to others.

20
Contributing to the World

Some children were playing below a guava tree. Two of them caught sight of the ripe guavas. They felled the guavas and shared them among themselves. You would have seen this typical incident perhaps with yourself or others during your childhood.

As a child, we would share and enjoy whatever we received with our friends. As we grew up, the thought of discrimination, "I," "me," "mine," began to dominate our thinking, and that childhood joy faded away

How was it possible for us during our childhood? It was because, as children we could easily regard everyone as a friend; no one was an outsider for us. But now, we consider everyone else except our direct family as outsiders. Even our cousins seem outsiders to many of us.

We need to get rid of these words, "other" and "outsider." We need to know the reality that there is no "other" in the world; we are all the varied expressions of oneness. This entire world is interconnected. There is no one separate here.

The sun that gives light and energy to countries all around the world is the same. The air that we breathe is the same. The sky that we gaze at is the same. We inhabit the same Earth without boundaries. Boundaries are the creation of human thought. Otherwise, there is an underlying oneness in everything that we all experience at a deep level.

When our faith awakens to the truth that we all are essentially one, it becomes easy for us to send healing rays to all. Many a time, some people feel, "It is okay to send healing rays to my family. But why should I send healing rays to my neighbor? What do I have to do with them?" If we understand that we are all an expression of God and that the same Consciousness pervades us all, then the feeling of "I, me, mine" will not prevail. Nothing will remain personal. The sending of healing rays will then become a natural and selfless deed.

When we lead a life with the belief "I am this body," our life becomes personal, limited, and self-centered; our actions lead to karmic disease. On the contrary, leading an impersonal life leads to liberation; it doesn't cause karmic bondage. Such a life brings superlative joy in our life and also becomes instrumental for relieving others of their bondage.

Most religious books refer to actions done to personally gain something as impious; such actions only create bondage. For example, if we love someone and expect the other person to reciprocate, even such love will cause bondage. When we love with the feeling that "All are One," that feeling makes our actions pious.

Our actions should be like that of a flower. When a flower renders fragrance, it neither desires anything in return nor does it favor anyone. It just spreads its fragrance without reservations. Even if someone plucks the flower, it spreads its fragrance to his hands. It doesn't differentiate between people.

Similarly, actions that are rid of desire are pious and righteous. They free us from karmic disease and help us lead an impersonal life. If we focus on the living presence that pervades everyone instead of focusing on the personal "I," then life becomes impersonal.

Due to ignorance, lowered awareness, and karmic disease, we begin to believe that selfless actions are a burden. In ignorance, we believe that we should perform every action for our own selfish sake just like everyone else. The truth is that our happiness lies in others' happiness. But today, people feel sad by seeing others' happiness. "Others have it, but I don't," this thought stops them from giving or sharing with others.

The energy that operates this entire world and gives thoughts to everybody, enabling them to perform actions, is one and the same. All these actions together take the world to the further stage of evolution. This means that every action performed by every being is an action in the service of that supreme power. Everyone's action is helping the world progress further. Then why not perform every action with an impersonal feeling? We can perform a small impersonal action of sending healing rays. This is an important step towards raising the level of global consciousness. We all need to take it on priority.

21
Self-healing Rays and Bright-healing Rays

We all go through both pleasant as well as unpleasant incidents in our life. We derive joy from a pleasant incident. However, some incidents are so frustrating that we spoil our relationships, health, and lose our peace of mind. Overwhelmed by emotions, we unknowingly invite negativity and place ourselves in problem situations. To put an end to this negativity and bring happiness in our life, we need to become benevolent. We need to forgive and send healing rays to ourselves and others in our life. It is only then that we can make our life fruitful and fulfilling.

We will now understand about an aspect of healing rays, which when adopted, can help us attain the ultimate goal of human life. We can play a significant role in creating a highly evolved society. For this, we need to render a selfless service of sending healing rays to ourselves and others. These healing rays are not ordinary healing rays but bright-healing rays, self-healing rays. Let us understand them in detail.

As we have already seen so far, healing rays are sent to bring about a healthy and positive change in people. Bright-healing rays are meant to wish benevolence for someone who pursues their highest possibility so that they attain their mission of human birth.

While sending bright-healing rays, we say, "May you attain your mission on Earth before the end of this embodiment. May your life dwell in the presence of God. May only God's will be fulfilled through your body without any interference of the ego."

We can wish such benevolence for someone only when we have understood this subject and are walking the path of Truth. If we are not clear about Mission Earth, how can we wish such benevolent feelings for others? We will send them healing rays only to fulfill their superficial needs. But when we gain the highest wisdom, we will pray for the fruition of the highest possibility in everyone's life. We will send bright-healing rays to them so that they achieve amazing, limitless, permanent bliss. To be able to send bright-healing rays to others, it is essential to first send self-healing rays to ourselves so that we progress on the path of the ultimate Truth.

Self-healing rays are the highest prayer that we offer for ourselves. The highest prayer in the world is for realizing our true nature, for knowing our mission on Earth and attaining it. Through self-healing rays, we move closer to experience the answer to "Who am I?" We have received this human body to discover the answer to this question experientially.

Mission Earth is the aim of discovering who we truly are and be established in that experience. We are not what we have believed ourselves to be. We believe we are the limited individual body. We identify with the body and further believe, "I am smart, I am clever, I am dark, or I am fair, I am a boy, or I am a girl, I am a Hindu, or I am a Christian," and so forth. Not just that, we tend to get attached to the objects and relationships that are associated with the body. We assume they are "mine." We say, "This is *my* brother, *my* mother, *my* father, *my* wife, *my* husband, *my* son, *my* daughter…" or "This is *my* car, *my* house, *my* mobile phone, *my* dress…" and so on.

The truth is that these are God's precious belongings that we only use temporarily. Even our body is not ours! That's also God's. When the time comes, we will need to give it off. "Nothing is ours" does not mean that we will not use anything. Instead, we will use everything with the right understanding, "This is God's precious belonging. While it is with me, I will use it happily." When we remember this in every incident, relationship, and while using any object, we will be relieved of the illusion of "I, me, mine" and will get over every sorrow. Then we will open up to the experience of who we truly are.

In truth, beyond the body, we are essentially the formless living presence, known by various names, like *Ishwar*, *Allah*, God, Consciousness, Lord, Self, and so on. We are the Self-witness, the Self-experience. We are Divinity in essence. The body is just a costume that has been placed over us, due to which we consider ourselves limited to our body.

Just like an island is in the middle of an ocean surrounded by water, our body stands like a pillar surrounded by the presence of God, the Self-experience, the ocean of Consciousness. The Self experiences Its own presence by using the pillar of the body as a pretext while the pillar exists. Even after the pillar falls, the Self is present but cannot experience Itself. During meditation, we experience our true nature—the limitless expanse of consciousness—by persistently enquiring within, "Who Am I?"

The extraordinary tree attained its highest possibility and became a human being. Similarly, our ultimate and highest possibility is to get established in our true essence. This highest possibility can be attained through self-enquiry on the question, "Who Am I?"

"Who am I?" is the greatest question on Earth because it leads us to our true Self and experience our beingness as soon as we ask this question. By repeatedly asking this question, we gain conviction that we are not this body. We turn within to experience our true Self. This question brings us to the realization of our true Self. All other questions connect us with the external world, but the question "Who Am I" unites us with our source. Attaining this experience is the final goal of human life, which makes life fruitful.

These days, most people are involved in the illusory world to such an extent that this question never occurs to them. The moment this thought arises within you, repeatedly ask the question to such an extent that you get that question to dominate your thinking, which will then connect you to your source. When you are connected with the source, every action will be selfless. Inculcate the habit of asking yourself, "Who Am I?" every hour. You can set an hourly reminder for this, like 01:01 p.m., 02:02 p.m., 03:03 p.m., and so on.

"Who am I?" is a self-healing ray that helps us return to our source. Therefore, to attain the ultimate purpose of our life, while sending healing rays to others, we should also send ourselves self-healing rays by enquiring into, "Who Am I?"

Whatever you invoke awakens within you. Invoke the consciousness that pervades everything, and it will awaken within and all around you. Invoke health, and health will begin to manifest in all. Whatever you invoke will grow and blossom. Therefore, first, invoke the Consciousness within you. Close your eyes for some time and bless your body; pray for it. Caress it and express your love, seek forgiveness, and then express gratitude.

Now, keep your eyes closed and express gratitude for every living being on Earth. Bring forth the following visual in your mind. Everyone is expressing the true Self according to the divine will and attaining contentment. This is the birthright of everyone. Everyone is enjoying this right. Everyone is attaining divine qualities like love, bliss, peace, perfect health, creativity, compassion, fulfillment, forgiveness, and playfulness. May everyone receive the knowledge of Truth and recognize their true nature. May everyone be established in the experience of the true Self. This is indeed happening.

Repeat the prayer, "O Lord, please lead us from darkness towards light and from light towards the divine light of consciousness. Please lead us from ignorance towards knowledge and from knowledge towards the divine wisdom of oneness—the supreme knowledge. Please lead us out of our beliefs towards Self-realization. Gratitude! Gratitude! Gratitude!"

22
Meditation to Transmit Healing Rays

Transforming oneself into one's pure divine nature is not easy. However, we automatically progress towards our divinity if we make ourselves the center of positive energy and shower healing rays on others. For this, we need to practice daily meditation to bring forth the divine light from within ourselves and radiate it all around us. We need to awaken to our true nature in meditation. For this, it is essential to close our eyes.

Most often, our awareness gets lost in worldly things when we move around in the world with open eyes. We see many things at once with open eyes making it difficult to focus our attention to meditate. It is essential to cut off from the world to meditate, and closing our eyes facilitates this. Our mind becomes peaceful and joyous with meditation, and when we brim with happiness, we begin to spread joy and happiness to others. Thus, we send healing rays to others.

Let us practice meditation to transmit healing statements. First, read the instructions for this meditation completely, understand, and then practice it step by step.

1. Sit in your preferred meditation posture and close your eyes.
2. Tell yourself, "I am going to transmit healing rays during this meditation."
3. Be relaxed. Inhale deeply and slowly exhale three times. Then continue breathing normally.
4. Now, imagine that you are getting filled with divine white light. Slowly, you reach a state where you are flooded with this light.
5. Remain in this state and feel that you have become the source of healing rays, which will be radiated from within you.
6. Now, first remember those people for whom you have harbored negative thoughts. Seek forgiveness from them. Then forgive those people who have misbehaved or thought negatively about you. You will begin to experience bliss in this process.
7. Then visualize those people who need inner strength. With a happy mind, repeat the following healing sentences that can render strength to them.
    - You are capable.
    - You are becoming successful.
    - Your every need is being fulfilled.
    - Be at peace; everything will be fine.
    - Relax.
    - Even this will pass away.
    - You are brimming with faith.
    - You are fully satisfied.
    - Your life is getting better and better.

8. Send healing rays with the faith that everything is good with the other person and he is capable of doing good for others.

9. Send healing rays for all the negative things happening in the world that come in the field of your awareness. Repeat the following lines in your mind –

10. May everyone be embraced by the healing rays of divine light.

11. May everyone seek refuge in the divine light.

12. May everyone come together and work for the wellbeing of one another.

13. May everyone contribute towards elevating the consciousness of the world.

14. Slowly open your eyes.

In this way, spread the vibrations of benevolent feelings all around so that positive energy reaches and heals all the negativity through healing rays. Besides this, the healing rays radiating through you will reach out to the world and establish truth, consciousness, and bliss.

By sending healing rays in this manner, you will experience yourself as the source of healing light.

With this meditation, you will feel healed by transmitting energy to others. You will feel more compassionate and energetic. By transmitting the power of these healing words, you will be able to make both your life and that of others bright and pleasant.

APPENDIX

Sending Healing Rays for Various Incidents

Opening Your Mind with Healing Rays

We go through various situations, deal with many people, and face several challenges during the day. Some make us feel pleasant, while some don't. Negative situations or conversations can adversely affect the mental and physical well-being of the people involved. Sending them healing rays can help them deal with the negativity.

While healing rays can be sent even in the middle of activity, it would be more effective if we take a pause and dwell in a meditative state for a couple of minutes to send healing rays. The meditative state helps us focus our mind, which then enhances the potency of the healing rays manifold.

To focus your mind, start by placing your attention on your breath during meditation. Witness each breath coming in, going out, pausing in between, and then continuing, as a spectator. Observe whether the breath is cold, warm, deep, or shallow. This will help you remain in the present—free from the pull of the past and future.

While sending healing rays to people, always ensure that you focus on what you want for them and not what you don't. For example, never verbalize, "Let them not face any trouble; nothing wrong should happen to them." Instead, say, "Let them always be safe and healthy."

Before sending healing rays to people, you must open your mind first. For that, you need to send healing rays to yourself first in the form of a prayer. This will help you become free from fear and raise your awareness, faith, purity of mind, and evoke love and benevolence for all beings within you.

Heartily accept, "All are pure and divine, I am also pure and divine," and extend these vibrations to one and all. There is no need to doubt: How can I be pure? Don't go by how you perceive your present state. Instead, focus on what you want to create for yourself and verbalize it in the present.

Sit straight with closed eyes in a comfortable meditative posture. Then verbalize the following healing sentences with courage:

> "O God, I am opening my mind so that it fills with benevolence for the entire world. Let my prayers touch everyone positively.

> "I am opening my mind so that it fills me with thirst for divine wisdom. Let my attainment of this wisdom bring wellbeing to everyone and awaken the divinity within them.

> "O God, I am opening my mind so that my awareness rises with every breath. Let my awareness be instrumental in bringing about everyone's betterment. Please help me with this.

> "I am opening my mind so that my confusion dissolves. Let my clarity benefit the growth of all. May everyone evolve.

> "O God, I am preparing myself for liberation, for emerging out of all mental

dilemmas. I am able to see everything clearly as it is. All my habits, tendencies, and ignorance are getting dissolved in the light of the Truth. Everyone is benefitting from my liberation.

"I am prepared to break free of all my fears. Fear blinds us from the Truth. However, all my fears are dissolving. My eyes are opening to the Truth. I am able to see the Truth in everything. Everyone is benefitting from my purity, serenity, and courage. Everyone is gathering strength to break free of their fears. Everyone is brimming with love, joy, courage, contentment, and health. Love, joy, and peace are spreading in every direction.

"O God, thank you so much for giving me yet another day to sing your praises. Bless my body with purity and sanctity so that it becomes a sacred temple of the divine Truth. Let the bells that ring in this temple in the form of thoughts that arise help raise faith and devotion in others. Thank you for fulfilling my prayers!"

With your eyes closed, let these feelings radiate in every direction in the form of divine white light. Visualize bright healing light being showered on Earth. Golden light, symbolizing heightened consciousness, is emanating from Earth, filling up the entire universe. There is love, joy, and peace everywhere.

In this way, by giving yourself healing rays every day, you will begin to experience these divine qualities unfold within you. With these feelings of benevolence, you will feel inspired to send healing rays to others. You will wish that everyone should experience this feeling of peace, contentment, and love.

INCIDENT 1

What to Do When You Are Anxious and Worried

Nitin went on a business trip for ten days to another city. As he couldn't complete his work in the stipulated time, his stay got extended by a couple of days. After finishing his work, he informed his wife, Neha, of his revised flight details and when he would reach home.

However, his flight got delayed for a couple of hours. But as his mobile phone was out of network coverage, he couldn't inform Neha about the delay.

At home, Neha started getting anxious and worried as he hadn't reached home on time, and his phone could not be reached. She got into a flurry of worrisome thoughts on the following lines:

- O God, what's happened? He should have been home by now. Is he facing any calamity?
- Don't know why his mobile phone is out of network coverage for so long. Where could he be? I hope nothing bad has happened.

- He should have at least informed me that he would get late. Whom do I ask now? Where do I look for him?

Parents experience similar feelings when their children go to school, college, a picnic, or a party. They keep worrying until their children return home.

If a survey were to be carried out, it would be observed that almost everyone is constantly worried about something or the other. But worrying does not solve the problem. Instead, it complicates the situation further.

Like Neha, usually, when one is worried, verbalizing such negative thoughts, keeps sending negative vibes to the other person. Instead, they should send healing rays in such situations. Every time a worrying thought arises, they should switch to sending healing rays. Deeper the worry, the stronger the healing rays! Instead of holding on to unnecessary worries, they should think positively and bless the other person.

Neha could have also thought on the following lines: "Maybe the flight has got delayed. Perhaps Nitin's mobile phone has got discharged. He could possibly be still in transit, and so his mobile is out of coverage," and so on. She needs to verbalize healing sentences and send healing rays to Nitin by choosing such thoughts.

Some examples of healing rays are:

- Everything is fine. You are God's favorite.
- You are an aspect of God. God's blessings are always with you.
- You are safely reaching home.
- You are safe and healthy.
- Nature takes care of one and all. It takes care of you too.
- You belong to God. So, no evil can touch you.
- Divine energy is spreading all around you, protecting and nourishing you.

INCIDENT 2

What to Do When You Are Gripped by Fear

Kiran went to a shopping mall along with her four-year-old son, Keval. As she was busy with shopping, somehow Keval got lost in the crowd. Kiran tried hard to search for him all around the mall but could not locate him.

A cold fear gripped her with the realization that she had lost Keval in the crowded mall. Scared and frantic, she started showing his picture on her mobile phone and asking all the passers-by whether they had seen him. When she called her husband, Kishor, and informed him about what had happened, he scolded her for her carelessness.

Instead of helping her and giving her courage, people around her kept talking about the worst possibilities, which further aggravated her fears. All sorts of negative thoughts arose in her mind. "I don't know where Keval must be! He could be crying! How can I find him in this crowd?! What if he has been kidnapped?! Where am I going to find him in this city?!"

She didn't realize that by entertaining such fearful thoughts, she was unknowingly sending negative rays to Keval. In such situations, no amount of worrying can improve the situation. Quite the contrary, the negative rays sent while worrying worsen the situation further.

Similarly, parents often find themselves worrying about their children's future. "Will my child get good education? What if they don't do well academically?! What if they need to stay away from home for their education? How will they manage on their own?" and so on.

If it's a girl child, then parents have different fears. They become worried about her safety and her marriage in addition to her career and financial wellbeing. "Will she find a good companion? How will her in-laws be? Hope she gets a good husband, and her in-laws treat her well. Hope she doesn't face any hardships there."

Besides such thoughts, some people also fear, "Nowadays, we cannot trust anybody," "Everyone needs money. If I lend money to someone today, will I get it back?" "If my children don't score good marks, they won't get a good job. How will they fulfill their dreams?"

In this way, people harbor a variety of fears and keep repeating negative statements. Instead, they need to face the fear themselves and free their children from it during such times. Otherwise, they unknowingly sow the seeds of fear in their children too. To safeguard yourself from this web of fear, you can send healing rays.

When you send healing rays, you can pray for the dissolution of fear in all the people in the world. Imagine divine white light showering on Earth, blessing everyone with courage and integrity. It is washing away all the fears in everyone. Everyone is living with faith and courage. With this imagination, repeat the following healing sentences:

- You can achieve your goal.
- May only goodness prevail.
- May your future be bright.

- May you receive everything according to God's will and your divine plan.
- You are born to lead a successful and fulfilling life.
- You are being supported by all, and you are a support to one and all.
- All are pure, and so are you.
- You are leading a courageous life.

INCIDENT 3
Healing Rays for Decision Making

Poonam had been staying in a joint family after her wedding. In the beginning, everyone behaved well with her. But after about two to three years, she started having conflicts with her in-laws. Her in-laws had their own set of problems. But Poonam was also equally responsible for the quarrelsome environment. She had no control over her anger and would blurt out words that would hurt her in-laws. Eventually, things came to such a point that her in-laws asked Poonam and her husband Pavan to move out and stay separately. So, they shifted to a new home with their two children.

Her in-laws would call her occasionally. They would also meet her at times during functions of mutual friends or relatives. Many years passed. One day, her in-laws felt apologetic about the way they had behaved with Poonam. They called Poonam and Pavan to stay over.

However, Poonam had not forgotten the way they had ill-treated her and her parents, the way they had humiliated her and asked her to leave the house. The thought of going back to them made her fume with rage. In this resentment, she paid no heed to her in-laws' request and decided not to go back. Nevertheless, she experienced inconvenience and dilemma while arriving at this decision.

We often find ourselves at such junctures when we need to make certain critical decisions that can make or break certain facets of our life. Some decisions are easy, while some are not. Sending ourselves healing rays can significantly help when we find ourselves in a dilemma about what direction we should take. If we see others struggling with a decision, we can send them healing rays too.

We can see the other person making a wrong decision in certain situations, which they don't realize. This is commonly seen in the case of parents and their children.

In such cases, parents grumble, "They don't want good advice. They will learn the hard way," "They have never made the right decisions in life." If parents decide for their children, the children grumble, "We have to suffer because of their wrong decisions," "They lived their life making their own choices, and now they don't allow us to live our way."

Now, the person making the decision is already in a dilemma. Why should we confuse him even more by thinking negatively about him? Instead of forcing our decision on him, we should first listen to his perspective, send him healing rays with benevolent feelings, and express our views to convey a higher understanding. This will help him make the right decision.

Some healing sentences that can help in such situations are:

- Let go of whatever has happened in the past. You are now competent to make the right decisions. You are more than capable of finding the right way for yourself.
- You are God's property, and you don't need to be scared. In case you commit any mistake, you can correct it.
- You are very thoughtful and considerate in making decisions.
- It is easy to learn the art of decision-making by making small decisions.

- With every decision, you are learning and progressing further.
- You are a part of the divine power of the Universe; hence your success is assured.
- You are sensible, loyal, and intelligent.
- You are sincere, truthful, and capable of making the right decisions.

INCIDENT 4
Healing Rays for Health

An elderly couple, Mr. and Mrs. Samuel, used to stay in an apartment. The gentleman was suffering from illness due to old age. One day, his health suddenly deteriorated further. His neighbor, a doctor, immediately called for an ambulance. As soon as the neighbors saw the ambulance enter the gate, they started having all kinds of negative thoughts.

This has been a familiar scene, especially during the COVID19 pandemic. Initially, people didn't have any information about the pandemic. But gradually, they were loaded with tons of information about it through the social media. People in every nook and corner started discussing it.

Although much of this information was hearsay and false alerts, most people fell prey to it. On top of that, people faced lockdowns, layoffs, and pay cuts. At one point in time, the whole world had come to a halt. This fueled the fear among the masses about their health and general wellbeing.

At such time, any sight of an ambulance also triggered negative thoughts in people. The negative thoughts could be like:

- Why has the ambulance come? It looks like they are taking the neighbor to the hospital. I hope it's not serious. Is he infected by that virus?
- So many people around the world are dying because of this pandemic! It's so scary to even think of what might happen in the near future!
- We're like sitting ducks in this lockdown. There seems to be no cure in sight either.
- There are so many people we know who are infected despite taking all precautions and staying indoors. Anyone can get infected anytime!
- Don't know how many more will fall prey to this pandemic!

Unfortunately, people are unaware of the ill effects of such thoughts. By obsessing over them, they only attract the undesirable and further intensify the already worsened situation. Every thought releases a certain vibration that attracts matching people, incidents, and situations. If we keep thinking about the disease, we will end up attracting more of it. The remedy is to focus on positive thoughts of health and wellbeing, and send healing rays to ourselves and others. Following are some of the healing sentences you can use:

- May the gentleman return home soon in a state of perfect health and fitness.
- May he become healthier than before after getting cured.
- Everyone is an embodiment of the same divine intelligence that renders every disease ineffective.
- Health and wellbeing are everyone's birthright. We all shall have it.
- Divine white light is showering on the patient, filling his body, his life, and his very existence with health and abundance.
- The patient is being treated by none other than God Himself. He is in the best hands!

- Every disease is preceded by its remedy. So, this is nothing new.
- May everyone be blessed. May everyone be uplifted.
- Everyone is attaining perfect health through natural remedies and medicines.
- May God bless both the patient and his loved ones with health and happiness.
- Divine white healing light is spreading to every corner of the world. Everyone is attaining perfect health by coming in contact with this light.
- May everyone be blessed with such divine wisdom that wipes out all their fears about disease.
- Having attained perfect health through positive vibrations, everyone is expressing their heartfelt gratitude to Nature.

INCIDENT
Healing Rays for Food

Food is an integral part of our life. We cannot sustain for very long without food. You may have heard, "Eat food with a peaceful mind and good feelings. Don't think ill of anyone while having food. Then that food will render you good health and keep you free from all diseases."

It is also an age-old practice to pray before having food so that the divine energy purifies and energizes it with positivity. It is said, "As your food, so is your mind, and as your mind, so is your body." This means, if our food is pure, so will our mind be pure, and if our mind is pure, so will our body be pure and healthy.

Praying is also a form of sending divine healing rays. When we serve food with a pure heart and a peaceful mind, they derive health and happiness. The same applies to the water we drink. If we pray for a few seconds before drinking water, the water gets purified and positively energized. We all know that more than 70% of our body comprises water. So, the water that we drink brings about an inner purification, the effect of which can be clearly seen on our face and body. It makes us feel healthy, enthusiastic, and positively charged.

Conversely, food cooked, served, or consumed with a troubled and distressed mind will have the converse effect. People may even verbalize negative words about the food being consumed, like, "This food is so bland. There is hardly any salt," "I just hate this dish. I always have an upset stomach after having it. I find it difficult to swallow it," "I'd rather eat at that restaurant than eat this!"

These statements are very common, but we don't know what effect they have in the unseen. The negative vibration of such words degrades the energy of the food and harms our health. Our feelings and thoughts about the food we eat can cause physical and mental sickness. Hence, sending healing rays to food while preparing or serving it turns it into nectar for all those who consume it. Thanking those who contributed their efforts to bring the food to our table and praying for their wellbeing is as good as sending healing rays. We can use the following healing sentences:

- O God, please bless the food we are about to eat.
- This food is filling my body and mind with divine energy.
- May this food be a source of good taste and good health to all those who consume it.
- Thank you,-God, for giving me hunger. Thanks to the farmer for growing the produce. Thanks to the traders for getting the food to me. Thanks to those who prepared the food.
- This water is purifying me within. I can feel its purity spreading as it flows within.
- Whatever I eat adds to my strength and stamina.
- Thank you God, for giving us hunger, food, and satisfaction from eating good food.

INCIDENT 6
Healing Rays for Anger

Akash threw open the door when he reached home and stormed in, frustrated and angered by something that had happened at work. The first victim of his anger turned out to be his five-year-old son, Amar, who was playing with his toys in the living room. "Look at the mess you've made." he bellowed, "Don't you have studies to finish? You keep playing all day long! Go to your room and start studying."

The next victim was his wife, Amita, as he entered the kitchen, "We have one kid, and you can't take care of him! What do you do all day?!"

Later in the night, when they all sat for dinner, he looked at the food on the table in disgust and said, "The same food every night! How can a man eat the same thing every single day of his life?! Is this the only dish you can cook?!" Saying this, he got up and stormed out of the kitchen without having eaten a single morsel, leaving behind a scared son and a deeply hurt wife. Sadly, this was a common occurrence in their home.

He would often pick fights with neighbors over petty issues. While driving, he would curse other drivers, "They have to park on both sides of the street! Where are we supposed to drive?! No one has the sense to drive a car these days! These people should be banned from getting their cars out on the road."

A lot of people get frustrated in traffic jams and give out negative vibrations, cursing everyone else. They often lose patience and get into arguments and fights. At work, people vent their anger and frustration on their colleagues and subordinates. Such people earn a bad reputation, and others tend to stay away from them. It is a natural human tendency to feel negative about people who are generally angry. The negative sentences could be:

- He has got into a habit of being angry all the time!
- She is never going to change. It's best to keep away from her!
- I don't think he does much else other than yell at others all day!
- Not a single day goes by without him getting angry at someone about something.
- He can't digest his food without getting angry.

By verbalizing or thinking this way, we send them negative vibrations that make them even more angry. At such times, we should understand that they are internally hurt and are masking their suffering with anger. It becomes our responsibility to send them healing rays to rid them of their pain and suffering.

Everybody likes a peaceful life. We generally seek relief from our anger and frustrations through outbursts or by indulging in exciting distractions, but these are only temporary means of escape. The permanent solution is to be entirely rid of them by freeing ourselves of the root cause of anger. Repeat the following healing sentences to wish such freedom and mental peace for everyone:

- You are becoming calm and peaceful.
- You are capable of patient and tranquil behavior.
- You can treat others with love, compassion, and empathy.
- You can gain control over your anger.
- You are channeling the power of your anger in the right direction and using it in creative endeavors.
- Love, peace, and joy are an integral part of your life.
- You are the source of patience and are full of creative energy.
- You are experiencing relief and supreme silence.
- Divine white light of peace and tranquility is being showered on Earth. Everyone is inviting peace into their life.
- Everyone is experiencing peace and bliss, and allowing peace to function in their life.

INCIDENT 7
Healing Rays for Problems

Jay had been planning to get married for a while but was not finding a suitable partner. He received many matrimonial alliances but couldn't make up his mind on any of them. This was causing him great distress.

One day he spoke to his uncle about his predicament. However, instead of being supportive and understanding, his uncle criticized him. "You'll never find someone satisfying all your criteria. I'm unable to understand what you are looking for in a life partner that's making it so difficult for you to decide. Now, set aside all your conditions. If you don't find a partner soon, you'll surely end up being a bachelor all your life!"

Jay was also going through financial challenges. When he spoke to his elder brother about it, his brother, too, instead of advising him, criticized him, "You keep shopping online, ordering food so often, making expensive trips, and enjoying parties every other weekend.

You are so extravagant and reckless. It's no wonder that you have holes in your pocket leaking money. You deserve it!"

In both these examples, Jay wanted solutions to his problems. But his uncle and brother, instead of helping him, criticized and blamed him. This complicated and worsened the problem in turn. Like Jay's uncle and brother, many people consider it their duty to criticize others for helping them out. They make critical statements like:

- You can never find a proper and lasting solution to any of your problems.
- I always see you wrestling with some problem or the other. You seem to be in love with problems!
- You always keep lamenting over some matter. You will never find peace.

We invariably connect with several people every day. To have a smooth life, we often face various challenges that become "problems" for us. Some problems are quite straightforward that we fix on our own. But, for the bigger and more challenging problems, we turn to our friends, siblings, parents, trusted relatives, mentors, and guides, whom we consider our well-wishers. We share our problems with them and expect the right advice and cooperation in turn.

Hence, whenever someone asks you for any help or advice, instead of criticizing or rebuking them, listen to them attentively, give them the right advice, and send them healing rays that will provide them with positive energy to solve their problem. They should feel optimistic after meeting you. The healing rays can be words like:

- May God bless you with the strength and wisdom to solve your problems.
- May God bless you with a smooth, peaceful, and happy life.
- You are capable of solving your problems the right way.
- We are always there to support you at every turn of your life.
- God's boundless grace is always showering on you.

Be independent, work in collaboration with others. But don't fall victim to others.

INCIDENT 8
Healing Rays for Inanimate Objects

Samir and Mihir were meeting each other after many years and catching up on how the last few years had been. Samir said, "You know, the house I'm living in now. It was such an unfortunate moment when I chose to buy such an ill-fated house! I've only met with bad luck ever since we moved in. In the very first week, there was a burglary. We lost nearly everything we had. Then my wife and son fell ill. No month goes by without the news of the death of some close acquaintance! I don't know what I should do!"

"That's really sad!" replied Mihir, "Strangely, I too am in a similar situation. I spent all my savings and bought this shop in a mall, thinking it would bring me good fortune. But ever since I moved my business here, I've had to put up with losses. Business is so bad here. I'm guessing the mall itself will shut down soon! This shop has gobbled up all my earlier profits and savings, everything I had!"

When people receive bad news, bear heavy losses, or face challenging situations, they blame it on other people or inanimate objects around them. They think negatively about their homes, businesses, jobs, vehicles, and so on. Their negative thoughts can be like:

- This (home, business, machine, office, shop, etc.) has brought me only misfortune. Ever since I bought it, I have only faced trouble and losses.
- This thing is a bad omen for me!
- Buying this was a waste of money! I should have bought something else.
- This machine has to always break down when I need it the most.

When we think negatively about inanimate objects, our vibrations affect them. You may have heard someone say, "I can never get your bike to start. Only you can do it!" or "I can never work on your laptop. God knows how it works for you!"

These are examples of how people are attuned to certain inanimate objects around them. When we speak, feel, or think positively about something, our vibrations affect our attunement with it. A certain machine may not work for anybody else but will work like a song for you. You may not consciously understand why, and you may even find it surprising.

All things in the universe, living or non-living, tangible or intangible, are constantly vibrating. Even objects that appear stationary are also vibrating. When we emit positive vibrations for something, it begins to resonate with our vibrations. Thus, by emitting positive vibes, we receive positive vibes in response. So also with negative vibes.

When we buy a new house, we invite people to a housewarming. We also celebrate some functions intermittently during the year so that people assemble and pray together. Their sacred positive vibrations help clean the atmosphere in the house. The house begins to resonate with a new auspicious frequency. This is one of the ways of sending healing rays to inanimate objects.

In India, our ancestors have set up the custom of worshipping machines, vehicles, and objects on the festival of Dussehra. They would treat the inanimate objects like living beings. During the

Diwali festival, we clean and decorate our homes and offices. All these are ways of sending healing rays to inanimate objects that are important in our lives. However, we don't have to wait for the advent of festivals to send them healing rays. We can begin right now and start improving our attunement with everything around us.

The healing sentences can be:

- May this home/ office be blessed with love, joy, peace, and prosperity.
- May this home/office always experience an abundant inflow of money.
- All the machines/ appliances/ equipment/ tools in this home/ office are in perfect attunement with me and flawlessly working.
- All my gadgets/ tools always support me.
- I am truly sorry for the way I have neglected or misused all the gadgets/ tools/ things in the past.
- I thank all my tools/ gadgets for making my life easy and comfortable.
- The same Consciousness exists in all inanimate objects as humans. We are all part of the Universal Consciousness.

INCIDENT 9

Send Healing Rays Instead of Blaming

Seema and Neeta had been collaborating on the same project for nearly a year. One day during a meeting, they had an arguement over an issue in the project. Their differences grew to such an extent that they stopped talking to each other and started working in isolation. Soon they even started bad-mouthing each other in front of others, which drove them further apart.

Many people tend to criticize, belittle, insult, and even bad-mouth others behind their back to prove themselves right. They fall prey to the compulsive behavior of bad-mouthing a third person when they meet someone. Whether it is a friend, a relative, a neighbor, a colleague, or the government, they derive an inexplicable sense of satisfaction in finding flaws in others and insulting them. They are least bothered about how their words and actions can affect others. Such people don't hesitate to even blame nature. Regardless of more or less rain, they always blame nature. Their negative sentences are like:

- The government bothers about satisfying citizens only during the period of elections, not otherwise.
- These days, everyone thinks they are too smart!
- People always misbehave with me. I feel the whole world is out to get me!
- Rain always plays spoilsport. It falls when we need it the least.

These days, it is difficult to find someone who has no expectations from anyone. Nearly everyone has some. When the other person doesn't fulfill their expectations or behave according to their will, they start finding faults with that person.

Parents also have several expectations from their children, like, they should excel at academics, excel at sports, win trophies, etc. When children fail to meet their expectations, parents unknowingly start underlining their faults. They complain, "It is more than enough for us if you study. How will you progress in life if you keep playing games on the mobile all the time? You just don't listen to us."

They don't understand that they are increasing their karmic disease with this behavior. Based on the extraordinary law of life, focusing on others' faults also attracts faults in their own lives. Therefore, instead of complaining, they should verbalize healing words like:

- You are surrounded by people of higher consciousness.
- You are an incarnation of divinity. God has no faults, and neither do you.
- You are a reservoir of divine qualities.
- We love and accept you just as you are.
- Everyone is a part of the same Consciousness. We all are pure and sacred.
- The world is full of good, kind, generous, and honest people like you.
- No one is at fault. All are faultless. All are incarnations of the Divine Self. I bow to all.

INCIDENT 10

Send Healing Rays to Yourself for Your Bad Habits

Sujit was feeling depressed these days. He fell into the wrong company and got into the habit of smoking. Having wasted his time in fun and frolic, he suffered badly at academics. Owing to his low scores, he couldn't receive any job offers. As his father had aged, the responsibility of earning a livelihood for his family fell upon him.

Despite trying hard, he couldn't find a job for himself. He started smoking even more in distress. Although he knew it was a harmful habit and wanted to get rid of it, he just couldn't do so. This badly affected his confidence and guilt began eating him within. Considering himself good for nothing, he began cursing himself and got terribly clouded with negativity.

Several teenagers and youngsters get trapped in the vicious cycle of addictions. They covertly do something wrong, unknown to their family. When they realize their mistakes later, they get consumed by fear, hopelessness, and guilt. When they find it difficult to overcome those addictions, they keep cursing themselves.

Some youth, unable to find a way out, lose their patience and get into the wrong ways of earning money. Their conscience reminds them what they are doing is not right, but they fail to mend their ways. Hence, they, too, fall prey to guilt.

Some people vent out their anger on others owing to their irritating nature. They repent later and blame themselves for their nature. As they fail to break free of this tendency, they feel frustrated, which leads to even more anger.

Such people usually keep repeating negative sentences either in their mind or verbally, like:

- I am useless, worthless, and good for nothing.
- I am a burden on my parents. My life is a waste.
- I am unable to control my anger. No one likes to be with me.

When people curse themselves in this manner, it is like shooting an arrow at oneself. By doing so, they intensify their karmic disease, which then aggravates their bad habits. If they intend to free themselves from their bad habits and self-sabotage, they need to stop shooting arrows at themselves first and begin sending healing rays to themselves. This will help them boost their confidence and positivity, and free them from fear, guilt, and hopelessness.

The healing sentences can be:

- I am a part of God. I need not be scared.
- As per my divine plan, everything that I need in life comes to me in perfect order at the right time. I need not harbor negative thoughts or deceive anyone.
- I am independent and self-sufficient. I can achieve whatever I want. I am receiving everything. Hence, there is no need to snatch anything from anyone.
- I am made in the image of God, and so, everything is possible for me.

- I am getting attuned to Nature. Now, I can be freed of all my bad habits and tendencies.

- I am receptive to divine qualities like love, joy, peace, purity, compassion, courage, abundance, and creativity. Only divine qualities are being expressed through me.

INCIDENT 11
Healing Rays for the World

Consider you are in bed and are about to sleep. Suddenly, you hear arguments in your neighborhood. You peep through the window and see two of your neighbors quarreling over something. You mentally blame them for disturbing the peace in the neighborhood and get back to bed.

Based on what we have understood so far, although you may have nothing to do with your arguing neighbors, you still need to send them healing rays so that their argument is sorted amicably at the earliest.

You may think, "I am not related to them in any way, nor to the topic of their argument. Then why should *I* send them healing rays?"

This is because the incident is transpiring in your field of awareness. Anything that happens in front of you or that you are informed about appears in your field of awareness. At such times, contribute positively by sending healing rays. If no bad news is received, the thought of sending healing rays will not occur to you at all. But if you come across any unpleasant incident or hear about some bad news, you need to send them healing rays.

Often, you read in the newspaper or watch on TV or social media about someone committing suicide, people dying in natural or manmade calamities, violence, terrorism, and so on. Sometimes you may not read or see the news yourself, but someone may inform you about it. In either case, send them healing rays. You may not know the victims personally, but since the incident has appeared in your field of awareness, you must send healing rays.

The healing sentences can be:

- You are safe. Your heart is the realm of forgiveness.
- There is purity in your thoughts and sweetness in your speech.
- Your life is a kingdom of love, joy, and peace.
- May God bless you and heal your life.

Today, owing to a lowered level of consciousness, the world is gripped by many problems like terrorism, epidemics, global warming, corruption, etc. When you discuss them with someone, you are indirectly energizing these problems through your attention. Instead, if you send healing rays, offer prayers, you help eradicate these problems and usher peace in the world.

In this way, when you take responsibility instead of criticizing, you stop being a part of the problem and become a part of the solution. You think in favor of others and do something for them. If not anything, you can at least transmit blessings, healing rays, benevolent feelings, white healing light, and healthy energy. These vibrations reach out to the entire universe and attract the most effective solutions. Without underestimating their importance, pray wholeheartedly every day. For this, you may take the help of the words given in the following prayers.

Healing Rays for World Peace

Close your eyes and visualize the globe. Imagine Divine white light showering all over the world and permeating all living beings. All negativity on Earth is dissolving on being touched by the white light. All beings on Earth are receiving this healing light. This light is pervading every human body, making it healthy. This divine white light is revitalizing every cell in every body. Everyone is collectively praying for the highest possibilities to manifest on Earth.

Everyone is joyous and healthy. All fears, worries, strained relationships, and financial problems are disappearing. Everyone is happy and content. The whole Earth is free from fear and greed, and everyone's level of consciousness has risen.

It feels like heaven has descended on Earth. A golden aura is emanating from Earth, symbolizing elevated consciousness. Divine white light showering from above and golden rays emerging from below—a beautiful confluence is happening on Earth. Love, joy, and peace prevail everywhere. Prayers that have been offered for centuries have finally come to fruition! Gratitude for all of this!

Healing Words for World Peace

May everyone on Earth be blessed with

divine wisdom, understanding, and the ultimate goal of life.

O God! Please free everyone from negative thoughts.

Please bless everyone with such purity and courage

that saves them from fear, greed, anger, hatred, and jealousy.

Please free those who are trapped in the dark hell of ignorance.

May everyone's level of consciousness rise high.

May Divine white light render perfect health to them.

May everyone receive adequate food and livelihood.

May divine white light reach everyone.

May everyone be blessed with healing rays,

abundant air, oxygen, clean water, and sunlight.

May everyone receive that which is required for their growth according to their Divine plan.

May everyone receive blessings that allow them to express their divine qualities.

May all beings on Earth be happy and healthy by Divine will!

Everyone is basking in the shower of love, joy, and peace, expressing Divine qualities.

Everyone in the world is becoming independent.

They are collaborating, helping, and serving one another with a feeling of gratitude.

May this collective prayer be offered by all and help the wellbeing and upliftment of all.

Everyone is returning to a state of higher consciousness.

I wish this from the bottom of my heart.

O God, Your will is getting fulfilled.

Thank you! Thank you! Thank you!

You can take the help of the above words to express your feelings. Repeat this prayer in your feelings, thoughts, words, and visuals. Keep repeating it mentally and transmit these vibrations in all directions.

Prayer for all the leaders of the world

1. All the leaders of the world, from various fields of activity (e.g., doctors, lawyers, engineers, politicians, police force, army) are all coming together and collectively working to solve every problem for the welfare of the world. They are aware that the welfare of people is their foremost responsibility. They are working together with unity in one direction for a selfless cause. The result of their magnanimous collaborative effort is divine and amazing. Their will is aligned with the will of God.

2. All the leaders are performing extraordinary feats. They are able to think out-of-box to arrive at the most suitable and effective solutions to the challenges in the world. As a result, all problems are getting eliminated.
3. All the leaders are peacemakers. They prioritize world peace above their ego. Keeping their personal gains aside, they care for the wellbeing of all. O God, may all such leaders be blessed with a noble mind, divine wisdom, and boundless energy to serve humanity.

Persistent collective prayer has the power of mass transformation. If the whole world were to come together at the same time and emanate the same prayer for just two minutes, a new level of wisdom would dawn in all of us.

A platform called **ANUPAM** has been initiated by Tej Gyan Foundation, where people pray at the same time for sending healing and awakening peace, wherever they may be, at any of the three scheduled time slots every day.

You can now register to join the ANUPAM fraternity and contribute your prayer for World Peace and Healing.

Visit: **https://tejgyanglobal.org/dhyanprarthanabeej**

or

Subscribe to: **"HAPPY THOUGHTS - PARAM GYAN"** channel on YouTube

PRAYER 1

Compassionate Wishes for Awakening

Let us express our compassion and shower bright-healing rays for the wellbeing of all. You can repeat the following prayer by visualizing people who need healing rays.

You are blessed… You are the life essence…

You are beyond all qualities… You are in perfect balance…

You are the One… You are the Supreme Self…

You are the witness to everything… You are the Self-witness…

You are an angel… You are Divine…

You are healthy… You are agile…

You are capable… You are fulfilled…

You are the Truth… You are self-willed…

You are truthful… You are blissful…

You are complete... You are happiness...

You are discerning... You are awareness...

You are absolute... You are goodness...

You are God's praise... You are the wealth of patience...

You are the Divine light... You are eternal life...

You are the Source of healing... You are the music of life...

You are the expression of love... You are joy and wonder ...

You are the divine presence... You are laughter...

You are serene...You are auspicious...

You are the only One... You are virtuous...

You are special... You are faith in action...

You are perfect... You are gratitude in action...

You are compassion... You are forgiveness...

You are prudent... You are pure consciousness...

There is purity in your thoughts... sweetness in your voice...

You are receptive... You are tolerant...

You are Divine ecstasy... You are Awakened...

You are a student of the Earth school...

You have learned your life lessons...

You are free from beliefs... You are untouched by the world...

You are blessed... You are the Supreme Self!

PRAYER 2

Compassionate Wishes for Wellbeing

May true benevolence prevail all over the world…
True benevolence… beyond auspicious and ominous…
May such benevolence touch every being…
May bright happiness prevail all over the world…
Bright happiness… beyond joy and sorrow…
May such happiness without reason fill every being…
May all fear fade away from the world…
May the lamp of courage be always lit…
May every fear fade away from within every being…
May bright love pervade the world…
Bright love… beyond hatred and attachment…
May such bright love awaken within every being…

May this life receive the ultimate grace…

May this life attain its ultimate goal…

May all beings be blessed!

Gratitude… Gratitude… Gratitude!

❑ ❑ ❑

You can send your opinion or feedback on this book to:
Tej Gyan Foundation, P.O. Box 25, Pimpri Colony,
Pimpri, Pune – 411017, Maharashtra, INDIA
Email: englishbooks@tejgyan.org

About Sirshree

Sirshree's spiritual quest, which began during his childhood, led him on a journey through various schools of thought and prevalent meditation practices. His overpowering desire to attain the Truth made him relinquish his teaching profession. After a long period of contemplation on the truth of life, his spiritual quest culminated in the attainment of the ultimate truth. Since then, over the last two decades, he has dedicated his life toward elevating mass consciousness and making spiritual pursuit simple and accessible to all.

Sirshree espouses, **"All paths that lead to the truth begin differently, but culminate at the same point – understanding. Understanding is complete in itself. Listening to this understanding is enough to attain the truth."**

Sirshree has delivered more than 3000 discourses that throw light on this understanding, simplify various aspects of life and unravel missing links in spirituality. He delivers the understanding in casual contemporary language by weaving profound aspects into analogies, parables and humor that provoke one to contemplate.

To make it possible for people from all walks of life to directly experience this understanding, Sirshree has designed the *Maha Aasmani Param Gyan Shivir* – a retreat designed as a comprehensive system for imparting wisdom. This system for wisdom, which has been accredited with ISO 9001:2015 certification, has inspired thousands of seekers from all walks of life to progress on their journey of the Truth. This system makes the wisdom accessible to every human being, regardless of religion, caste, social strata, country or belief system.

Sirshree is the founder of Tej Gyan Foundation, a no-profit organization committed to raising mass consciousness with branches in India, the United States, Europe and Asia-Pacific. Sirshree's retreats have transformed the lives of thousands and his teachings have inspired various social initiatives for raising global consciousness.

His published work includes more than 150 books, some of which have been translated in more than 10 languages and published by leading publishers. Sirshree's books provide profound and practical reading on existential subjects like emotional maturity, harmony in relationships, developing self-belief, overcoming stress and anxiety, and dealing with the question of life-beyond-death, to name a few. His literature on core spirituality expounds the deeper meaning of self-realization and self-stabilization, unravelling missing links in the understanding of karma, wisdom, devotion, meditation and consciousness.

Various luminaries and celebrities like His Holiness the Dalai Lama, publishers Mr. Reid Tracy, Ms. Tami Simon and Yoga Master Dr. B. K. S. Iyengar have released Sirshree's books and lauded his work. "The Source" book series, authored by Sirshree, has sold over 10 million copies in 5 years. His book, "The Warrior's Mirror", published by Penguin, was featured in the Limca Book of Records for being released on the same day in 11 languages.

Tejgyan... The Road Ahead
What is Tejgyan?

Tejgyan is the wisdom of the existential truth, which is beyond duality. "Gyan" is a term commonly used for "knowledge". Tejgyan is the wisdom beyond knowledge and ignorance. It is understanding that arises from direct experience of the final truth. It is what sets us free from the limitations of the mind and opens us to our highest potential.

In today's world, there are people who feel disharmony and are desperately trying to achieve balance in an unpredictable life. Tejgyan helps them in harmonizing with their true nature, the Self, thereby restoring balance in all aspects of their lives.

And then, there are those who are successful, but feel a sense of emptiness within. Tejgyan provides them fulfilment and helps them to embark on a journey towards self-realization. There are others who feel lost and are seeking the meaning of life. Tejgyan helps them to realize the true purpose of human life.

All this is possible with Tejgyan due to a very simple reason. The experience of the ultimate truth (God or Pure consciousness) is always available. The direct experience of this truth is possible provided the right method is known. Tejgyan is that method, that understanding.

The understanding of Tejgyan makes it possible to lead a life of freedom from fear, worry, anger and stress. It helps in attaining physical vitality, emotional strength and stability, harmony in relationships, financial freedom and spiritual progress.

At Tej Gyan Foundation, Sirshree imparts this understanding through a System for Wisdom – a series of retreats that guides participants step by step towards realizing the true Self, being established in the experience of self-realization, and expressing its qualities. This system for wisdom has been accredited with the ISO 9001:2015 certification.

Maha Aasmani Param Gyan Shivir

"**Maha Aasmani Param Gyan Shivir**" is the flagship Self-realization retreat offered by Tej Gyan Foundation. The retreat is conducted in Hindi. The teachings of the retreat are non-denominational (secular).

This residential retreat is held for 3 to 5 days at the foundation's MaNaN Ashram amidst the glory of the mountains and the pristine beauty of nature. The Ashram is located at the outskirts of the city of Pune in India, and is well connected by air, road and rail. The retreat is also held at other centres of Tej Gyan Foundation across the world.

You can participate in this retreat to attain ageless wisdom through a unique System for Wisdom so that you can:

1. Discover "Who am I" through direct experience.
2. Learn to abide in pure consciousness while functioning in the world, allowing the qualities of consciousness like peace, love, joy, compassion, abundance and creativity to manifest.
3. Acquire simple tools to use in everyday life, which help quiet the chattering mind.
4. Get practical techniques to be in the present and connect to the source of all answers within (the inner guru).
5. Discover missing links in the practices of Meditation (*Dhyana*), Action (*Karma*), Wisdom (*Gyana*) and Devotion (*Bhakti*).
6. Understand the nature of your body-mind mechanism to attain freedom form its tendencies.
7. Learn practical methods to shift from mind-centered living to consciousness-centered living.

A Mini-retreat is also conducted, especially for teenagers (14 to 16 years of age) during summer and winter vacations.

To register for retreats, visit www.tejgyan.org, contact (+91) 9921008060, or email mail@tejgyan.com

About Tej Gyan Foundation

Tej Gyan Foundation (TGF) was established with the mission of creating a highly evolved society through all-round development of every individual that transforms all the facets of their lives. It is a non-profit organization, founded on the teachings of Sirshree.

The Foundation has received the ISO certification (ISO 9001:2015) for its system of imparting wisdom. It has centres all across India as well as in other countries. The motto of Tej Gyan Foundation is 'Happy Thoughts'.

At the core of the philosophy of Tejgyan is the Power of Acceptance. Acceptance has profound meaning and is at the core of our Being. It is Acceptance that brings forth true love, joy and peace.

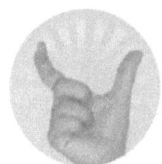

Symbol of Acceptance

The Symbol of Acceptance – shown above – is a representation of this truth. The symbol represents brackets. Whatever occurs in life falls within these brackets that signify acceptance of whatever is. Hence, this symbol forms the centerpiece of the Foundation's MaNaN Ashram.

The Foundation is creating a highly evolved society through:
- Tejgyan Programs (Retreats, YouTube Webcasts)
- Tejgyan Books and Apps
- Tejgyan Projects (Value education, Women empowerment, Peace initiatives)

The Foundation undertakes projects to elevate the level of consciousness among students, youth, women, senior citizens, teachers, doctors, leaders, professionals, corporate and Government organizations, police force, prisoners etc.

SELECT BOOKS AUTHORED BY SIRSHREE

   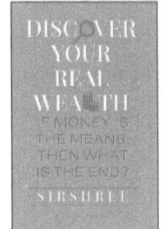

 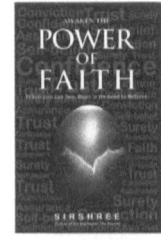  

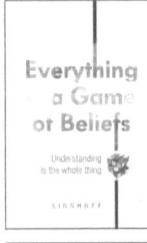   

To order these and other books authored by Sirshree
Visit **www.gethappythoughts.org**

Good News!

Maha Aasmani Param Gyan Retreat
is now conducted ONLINE in Hindi!

You can participate in the retreat from the convenience of your home. The retreat is conducted in 3 parts during weekends:

1. The Foundation Truth retreat

2. The Bright Responsibility retreat

3. The Maha Aasmani final retreat

For more details, please call: +91 9921008060, +91 9921008075

To register, visit: https://www.tejgyanglobal.org/mareg

Books can be delivered at your doorstep by registered post or courier. You can request the same through postal money order or pay by VPP. Please send the money order to either of the following two addresses:

WOW Publishings Pvt. Ltd.

1. Registered Office: S. No. 1A, Irani Market, Building No. D-38, Yerawada, Pune – 411006.

2. Post Box No. 36, Pimpri Colony Post Office, Pimpri, Pune - 411017

Phone No: (+91) 9011013210 / 9623457873

You can also order your copy at the online store:

www.gethappythoughts.org

*Free Shipping plus 10% Discount on purchases above Rs. 500/-

For further details contact:
Tejgyan Global Foundation
Registered Office:
Happy Thoughts Building, Vikrant Complex, Near Tapovan Mandir, Pimpri, Pune 411017, Maharashtra, India.
Contact No: 020-27411240, 27412576
Email: mail@tejgyan.com

MaNaN Ashram:
Survey No. 43, Sanas Nagar, Nandoshi gaon, Kirkatwadi Phata, Sinhagad Road, Tal. Haveli, Dist. Pune 411024, Maharashtra, India.
Contact No: 992100 8060.

Hyderabad: 9885558100, Bangalore: 9880412588,
Delhi : 9891059875, Nashik: 9326967980, Mumbai: 9373440985

For accessing our unique 'System for Wisdom' from self-help to self-realization, please follow us on:

	Website Online Shopping/ Blog	www.tejgyan.org www.gethappythoughts.org
	Video Channel	www.youtube.com/tejgyan For Q&A videos: http://goo.gl/YA81DQ
	Social networking	www.facebook.com/tejgyan
	Social networking	www.twitter.com/sirshree
	Internet Radio	http://www.tejgyan.org/internetradio.aspx

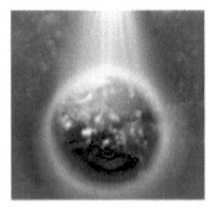

Pray for World Peace along with thousands of others every day at 09:09am and 09:09pm

Divine Light of Love, Bliss and Peace is Showering;
The Golden Light of Higher Consciousness is Rising;
All negativity on Earth is Dissolving;
Everyone is in Peace and Blissfully Shining;
O God, Gratitude for Everything!

www.ingramcontent.com/pod-product-compliance
Lightning Source LLC
LaVergne TN
LVHW041847070526
838199LV00045BA/1481